TOUGH TRUTHS FOR TODAY'S LIVING

D. STUART BRISCOE

TOUGH TRUTHS FOR TODAY'S LIVING

WORD BOOKS
PUBLISHER
WACO, TEXAS

A DIVISION OF
WORD, INCORPORATED

First Printing—June 1978
First Paperback Printing—October 1984

TOUGH TRUTHS FOR TODAY'S LIVING

Formerly published under the title,
Now for Something Totally Different

ISBN 0-8499-2999-7
Library of Congress Catalog Card Number 77-92474

Printed in the United States of America

Contents

Introduction

When Jesus Christ arrived on the scene about two thousand years ago it was easy to see he was different. He had a delightful capacity for living among the men and women of his day feeling their sorrows, enjoying their triumphs, yet avoiding their excesses and refuting their errors. He was thoroughly alive and alert, critical yet compassionate. Whether people were rich or poor appeared to concern him not at all. He seemed at ease in the midst of a group of belligerent theologians, coarse soldiers, or desperate sufferers. Composed, articulate, tough yet tender, he strode across a tiny corner of our world for a little over thirty years and our world has never recovered from his visit.

The quality of his different life was matched only by the caliber of his shattering teaching. Living as he did in a society uniquely rooted in tradition, he didn't hesitate to expose and explode cherished ideas where he felt such action was justified. He was death to duplicity; he hated hypocrisy. Yet he never stooped to being destructive and negative—for one reason: He had come to reveal the truth of God through his life and his lips. This truth challenged error at every point, it exposed sin in every form, and where it challenged and exposed it invariably changed and recycled. Those who heard him and followed him in discipleship became different as he was different.

Contemporary society needs change to survive. Its attention span is so short it is bored in minutes. Its appetite for the thrilling and the different is so insatiable that it lurches from madcap scheme to ludicrous philosophy with alarming momentum. But with the change comes the decay, and through the decay spreads the disintegration. Change for the sake of change changes nothing other than the cover under which the decay of change continues. If only something different could be found that would not accelerate disintegration of life and society. Perhaps if Christ could come back he could do something.

Idle thoughts? Not at all. For while he left for heaven and promised to return, he is resident in our society through his body the church. He is here to be as different as he always was, but you would not always know it. Why? For him to be seen in all his difference requires a church that is different from society—because it is composed of people who are different. And the difference of the church and the Christian is determined by the degree in which both live in obedience to his different teachings and reflect the dynamic of his indwelling presence.

In short, his disciples need to sit again at his feet and hear his word. That will make a difference in them so radical that they will be different in their world which will be changed because they passed through. I know of no better place to start than on the Mount where the Sermon that was different was preached.

1

The Christian
and Conduct

I believe this book is timely because there is so much public confusion as to what basic moral and ethical standards really are. This is true not only on the personal, individual level, but we are seeing moral and spiritual confusion on the national and international level as well. Many people are asking, how are we supposed to behave? Where do we find a moral code to live by? Where do we get the power and ability to live up to the moral and ethical standards that we have ourselves accepted?

I believe the Lord Jesus has anticipated our questions and has already given us the answers in his discourse known as the Sermon on the Mount. In it he expressed principles—moral, ethical, and social—that come from his eternal mind and have to do with men and women of all ages. These principles are tremendously relevant to people who are in the kingdom. But just one word of warning here. Jesus' teachings given in the Sermon on the Mount were given to his disciples. They were not broadcast generally. One of the problems we have is that we try to get a fallen society to behave as if it were made up of Christians. Now that's something we will never do. Our big problem is not getting fallen society to behave like Christians. The big problem is to get Christians to stop behaving like fallen society! If we could only get Christians to act like

11

Christians, we would discover that the principles enunciated here produce a totally different moral, ethical, and social standard, making Christian behavior distinctive and unlike that of the rest of the world. In the Sermon on the Mount, Jesus is telling his disciples, "Now look. If you're really going to be my men and my women, you're going to be bucking the rest of society in just about every conceivable area."

One of the tragedies to befall our nation and other nations is this: Christians have lost their distinctiveness. Because they have, and because they have failed to be what God intends them to be in any society, society as a whole has lost the Christian voice. As a result, society has lost its salt, its guiding light. It has lost its city set on a hill, the example that Jesus said Christians were to be. Perhaps the way to national revival is not to try to superimpose upon a lost society principles that they will never be able to accept. Rather, the way to national revival is to get Christians once again to begin to adhere to the social, moral, and ethical standards set forth in the Sermon on the Mount, the norm for Christian experience in the midst of a lost society. Perhaps then once again we will begin to produce Christians who buck the stream, Christians who are a thorn in the flesh to a system that is godless. Once again the Christians will become what they were intended to be —the salt of the earth, the city set on a hill, the light on a candlestick. And maybe then once again society will begin to see the effectiveness of the ministry of Jesus Christ.

As we take an overview of this matter of Christian conduct, we're going to look at the dynamics of human behavior. Then we'll think about the difficulties of human behavior. Finally, we will discuss the distinctives of Christian behavior.

The Dynamics of Human Behavior

First, let's look at the dynamics of human behavior. There are three areas involved in the behavior mechanism of a normal human being. We all have *motivational forces,* and superimposed upon our motivational forces are certain *moral factors.* And usually these motivational and moral factors are to a large extent in opposition to each other. At this point a third factor comes into play: the *mechanism for choice.* This choice mechanism is the referee. It keeps the other two opposing factors at arm's length and makes them complementary rather than competitive.

Motivational forces have to do with the self. Unfortunately, in evangelical Christianity the term self usually has a bad connotation. But self is not necessarily bad. For example, Jesus tells us that we are to love our neighbor as ourselves (Matt. 19:19), so obviously self-love is a biblical concept. In God's eyes his children are important—they have worth. There is a divine dimension in each of us. As we begin to see this eternal evaluation of the human being, we discover certain elements which God has put into us, basic natural motivational forces. Three of these are: self-preservation, self-gratification, and self-glorification. Almost automatically we react negatively to these terms. They're all bad. Anyone interested in self-preservation, self-gratification, or self-glorification is sinful. Not necessarily. They are part of the built-in motivational mechanism that is necessary to make us behave as human beings.

For instance, when a baby begins to crawl around and touches something hot, what happens? The very first time a baby is introduced to a fire, he learns something. He learns that fire burns. What is built into a baby's mind as a result of that little burned hand? He learns a certain fear of fire. This is what we call self-preservation, a basic motivational factor.

There is a second motivational force—self-gratification. When a little baby is born, what does he or she do quite soon? The baby demonstrates an insatiable desire for food. This is a form of self-gratification known as hunger. This desire for self-gratification is tremendously important. If the baby didn't have it, he'd starve. There would be no way the baby could survive without this in-born motivation. If we didn't have certain self-preservation motivational factors, we would not survive in a basically hostile world. These are survival mechanisms. They're all an inherent part of our behavior.

The third motivational force is self-glorification. This, too, is evidenced quite early in life. A baby soon learns he can get attention by opening his mouth wide and yelling at the top of his voice. In fact, he will probably pull every trick in the book to make absolutely certain he gets all the attention possible!

And that's perfectly natural. Babies need this instinct to survive as well.

Obviously, all these basic motivational forces in human behavior produce individual drives. They produce a person who's going to look out for number one. *I've* got to survive. *I've* got to be kept out of danger. *I* must have shelter. *I* cannot survive without warmth. *I* must have love. And so it goes. Without these drives mankind wouldn't and couldn't survive.

It's also perfectly obvious where those demands can lead us. That's why God has also equipped us not only with motivational forces, but also with moral factors. The moral factors built into human beings may also be classified under three headings. First of all, the conscience is a built-in factor. In his Epistle to the Romans, Paul points out that there are certain concepts common to all mankind (Rom. 1:18ff.). There is a law written in people's hearts. Many people consider this sensitivity to God's law to be the conscience. Every human being has a certain conscience. As a baby begins to grow, he finds himself in conflict with certain basic egocentric drives. Because he is a member of a civilized society, some of these basic drives cannot be exercised to the full. The growing person begins to discover that he has to live not only in terms of himself, but, in terms of other people as well. Through these overall controlling forces, conscience begins to work. And conscience begins to flash a warning light whenever the young person violates the rights of others in his drive to satisfy his own desires. Basic motivational drives are being tempered by basic moral factors, and the still small voice of conscience is beginning to speak.

In addition to the effect of moral factors upon the conscience, community thinking also comes into play. Those of us who travel widely notice how community thinking varies from place to place. As you wander around the world and see the differences in people's behavior patterns, you begin to understand that the differences in behavior patterns are developed through variations in community thinking. Consider how community thinking varies from the inner city to suburbia in the same area. It differs even more markedly between countries, and between geographic areas like the Middle East and the Far East. Wherever you go you will find that communities think in totally different ways. We in the United States consider ourselves as highly civilized, more so than most other parts of the world. But are we?

I was in South America not long ago and spent some time with one of the primitive tribes. This tribe had an interesting custom, too interesting for me to share in complete detail! Let me just give you a broad overview. In that tribe when a girl arrived at the age of puberty, she climbed a tree. Since the area was rather barren, there weren't many trees, so she was immediately noticeable! In case she wasn't noticed, she sang. I don't know the exact words of the song, but the message was basically, "I'm available." This was what she sang from the top of her tree.

Naturally, the men of the tribe responded positively to her message, and they began to appear from all points of the compass. The law of the tribe was simple: she belonged to the first guy to pull her down out of the tree! Again quite naturally, children were born of the resulting union. The tribal law stipulated that when children were born as a result of this alliance, it was incumbent on the parents to establish a home for the child—or the infant must be killed. The couple could go through this over and over again as children were born out of this "alliance" (which was perfectly legitimate by community standards).

Then one day the couple could decide they wanted to be regarded as married. They could announce their decision by keeping a child. The first child kept was evidence that now they were married. At that point stringent community regulations came into effect. Now certain rules against adultery prevailed. If any married person committed adultery in that tribe, then the chief could slash open the back of his neck with the "adulterer's knife" kept specifically for that purpose. This is an example of the community thinking of a primitive Indian tribe.

Notice the similarities between that tribe and so-called civilization today. Plenty of our young ladies today go around announcing, "I am available," once they have reached the age of puberty or slightly older. They don't climb trees, they just dress that way. They don't sing songs, they just announce it in other ways. The message is unmistakable to any male with his eyes open. The message is loud and clear: "I am available." They're as civilized as that primitive tribe in the South American jungle. Only we've gone a little bit further now—unwanted offspring from this alliance can be done away with. They don't bury the babies alive as the Indian tribe does. They simply abort them. Our principle of operation in so-called civilization is actually worse than the principle of operation in the primitive society. The difference is simply this: They have an "adulterer's knife" and we don't. We condone adultery. I have said all this to make a point: We need to be very careful when we evaluate other community standards of behavior. In many instances, our so-called civilization is drastically uncivilized in comparison with even the most primitive tribes.

If a person is going to behave in a normal pattern, these motivational forces in him must be controlled to a certain extent by moral factors. These moral factors are built up as a result of inbred conscience, community thinking, and then thirdly, convictions that are introduced. This is where we parents come in. God gave children to us to raise. One of the major breakdowns in society today is right at this point: the total failure of the home to introduce valid convictions which in turn produce moral factors to control motivational forces.

There is a third element involved in the dynamics of human behavior, and that is the mechanism of choice. We have seen two drives at work: the motivational forces and the moral factors. What happens when the drives for self-gratification, self-glorification, or self-preservation are such that a person's moral principles are in total opposition? A conflict arises, and the outcome of that conflict is determined by the mechanism of choice given to every human being by God. The mechanism of choice is the ability to discern a valid motivational force and a valid moral factor. The mechanism of choice gives me the ability to discriminate and discern between what is a valid moral principle and what is a totally amoral principle. I then begin to make decisions. Every decision is a product of discernment and discrimination. It isn't really surprising to me that our human behavior in today's world has gone berserk. Often we human beings haven't even tried to understand what really is involved in the dynamics of human behavior.

The Difficulties of Human Behavior

We've looked at the dynamics of human behavior, so now let's examine the difficulties of human behavior. These are caused mainly by unrestrained motivational forces. If the forces of self-preservation, self-gratification, and self-glorification are unrestrained, terrible difficulties in human behavior will emerge. Think of the businessman plagued by this problem of self-preservation. The one thing he is interested in is preserving his position. Morality does not matter. The only thing that matters to him is his own survival and success—at any price. This is one of the main causes of our problems in American and Western European society today. In many cases, we have a business ethic that is nothing more than unrestrained motivational forces operating for self-preservation. In the business world, this kind of attitude in management generates the same reaction in employees. They band together to form a union, and they elect a fiery negotiator to represent them. What is his main interest? Self-preservation. In the resulting battle, industry begins to come apart at the seams. Why? Because of unrestrained motivational forces—people convinced that self-preservation is all that matters.

Now let's add the urge toward self-gratification. If a person is mainly concerned with gratifying himself, then he is not really going to be careful about how he gets his gratification. The important thing is that it "pleases me." In our Western civilization we are producing people who have been taught that anything is legitimate if it gratifies "me." Morality and motivation do not matter as long as I am satisfied.

This is where the church of Jesus Christ is supposed to speak out loud and clear. Christians are to warn our world: "Look, one of our major problems is this: our lax moral standards are allowing chaos to enter and operate in our society. That's why humanity is where it is." History reveals that the church sometimes goes overboard and overreacts against moral standards that are weak. Often in reaction the church produces too stringent a moral standard, confusing and alienating the world around it. So it is possible to get into difficulties either way, whether the motivational forces are unrestrained or the moral factors are unsatisfactory.

I don't believe our major problem in society is either of these two; our major problem is, rather, simple mechanical breakdown. The three dynamics (motivational, moral, and mechanical) all have the same potential failure. Obviously, the moral can go wrong. So, too, can the motivational. But the mechanism of choice is the area usually overlooked today. And it is here that we need to be fully alert and alive. In Romans 7 Paul writes about the sort of confusion that exists in a person's life if his motivational and moral forces are battling, and he is incapable of making a choice through the mechanism God has given him. Paul says, "For the good that I would, I do not: but the evil which I would not, that I do" (Rom. 7:19). A person in this bind wants to do a certain thing, but he knows it is wrong. Here we see the motivational battling with the moral. This is humanity's major problem: an impasse between the unrestrained motivational forces and uneducated moral factors which is not adequately resolved because we have a mechanism of choice incapable of making the right decisions.

Ungodly people have never had the spiritual experience necessary to equip them to discern and discriminate and decide correctly. This is where the distinctiveness of Christian behavior comes in. True Christianity demands a standard of behavior above and beyond that which society has decided is normal. As we look further into the Sermon on the Mount, you will begin to see what I mean.

The Distinctives of the Christian's Behavior

Let me just point out four distinctives of Christian behavior that we find in this introduction to the Sermon on the Mount. First of all, there's the matter of *morality*. If there's going to be a distinctive Christian behavior, there is going to be a distinctive *Christian* morality. Underline this thought. Many different moral systems are abroad today. You can divide them into two main groups. One school of thought is based on speculation, human speculation, the result of man sitting down here scratching his head trying to figure out which way to go. The other school of thought or system is based on divine revelation. God speaking from heaven is saying, "This is the way.

Walk ye in it." The two systems are in total conflict. One section of society is saying, "Where on earth are we going?" The result is speculative philosophy—that produces speculative morality—that produces speculative disaster. At the same time God is saying, "This is the way. Walk ye in it." When Jesus sat on his mountaintop, gathering his disciples around him, he was saying, "Fellows, listen to me. Don't listen to the world around you. Simply listen to me. I am going to reveal to you a system of morality that is workable."

The morality that works has to come from mountain revelation, not from human speculation. As Christians our norm for behavior must come from God. Any Christian who tries to operate on society's behavior patterns had better recheck his Christianity. His morality must come from above. His ethics, his morals, his behavior patterns are to be found in the Word of God.

Secondly, it's a matter of *mentality*, a matter of learning at Jesus' feet. This is what the disciples did. Matthew sets the scene: "Seeing the multitudes, he went up into a mountain: and when he was set, his disciples came unto him: And he opened his mouth, and taught them" (5:1,2). Behavior comes from mentality, and mentality is set alight by the teachings of Jesus Christ. The eternal principles he enunciated are the bases of distinctive Christian behavior. We have a mentality that comes from above, from Jesus Christ himself. We do not learn from *experiment* along with the rest of the world, but from *exposition* that comes from the Lord of glory.

The third distinctive is a matter of *mastery*. We Christians are not supposed to be on an ego trip. We are to be disciples. Jesus said, "Discipleship is simply this. You take up your cross and follow me daily. If you live your own life, you'll lose it. But if you lose your life in mine, you'll find it." That is the attitude of surrender that is the total antithesis of the ego trip.

Much that passes for Christianity today is nothing more than glorified human speculation, I'm afraid. It is nothing more or less than worldly experimentation. It is nothing more or less than a glorified evangelical ego trip. This is our problem. We need a new morality, a new mentality, a new mastery. This is the basis of distinctive Christian behavior.

And finally, it's a matter of *minority*. I get a great kick out of the Lord Jesus seeing the multitudes and calling twelve men to one side. He said, "Fellows, see that multitude? Let's hit the multitude." How is he going to do it? By getting a nucleus, a minority. He is going to work with the minority to change the majority. I may be rather cynical, but I think the multitude is very often wrong. This may run contrary to your political thinking, but I believe it. What a delightful thing it is to be a Christian, knowing you're always going to be in the minority. And you know, it takes a certain kind of minority thinking to produce distinctive Christianity. That's what we're after.

2

The Christian
and Happiness

A divine minority against a secular majority. This is the way I
would describe what it means to be a distinctive, dynamic,
supernormal Christian in our modern-day society. Jesus had
some words for us in Matthew 5:

> Blessed are the poor in spirit: for theirs is the kingdom of
> heaven.
> Blessed are they that mourn: for they shall be comforted.
> Blessed are the meek: for they shall inherit the earth.
> Blessed are they which do hunger and thirst after righteous-
> ness: for they shall be filled.
> Blessed are the merciful: for they shall obtain mercy.
> Blessed are the pure in heart: for they shall see God.
> Blessed are the peacemakers: for they shall be called the chil-
> dren of God.
> Blessed are they which are persecuted for righteousness' sake:
> for theirs is the kingdom of heaven.
> Blessed are ye, when men shall revile you, and persecute you,
> and shall say all manner of evil against you falsely, for my sake.
> Rejoice, and be exceeding glad: for great is your reward in
> heaven: for so persecuted they the prophets which were before
> you (vv. 3–12).

As Jesus begins to teach his disciples, what is the very first word he utters? It is the word "blessed." He doesn't just say it once; he repeats it a total of eight times. I think he meant for us to take particular notice of it! The word "blessed" is a rather lovely word often used by us without our really understanding what it means. In the Greek it is *makarios*. The Greek people thought their gods had it made, and they used the word to describe this unbelievable state of well-being in which the gods lived. This is the word used by the Lord in the New Testament as he begins to describe the life he has come to give to his people. He has come to give them a life of blessedness.

Makarios living is what Jesus has in mind for his people. He wants us to live in a state of contentment, a state of fulfillment. We are to live in a state of happiness, a state of joy. As I look around me in the church, I think in some instances we have lost this message. The church has become involved in many areas of ministry, but I'm afraid we've forgotten that the Lord Jesus came to earth to instill unbelievable blessedness, *makarios*, in people's lives.

This should not surprise us. When Paul wrote to Timothy, he called God "the blessed God" (1 Tim. 1:11). This concept of God is not difficult to grasp. We can picture him as contented, fulfilled, and complete. We have no difficulty thinking of God as being fulfilled, as being complete. But do we ever think of God as being happy? God is in essence happy, joyful. He is in essence *makarios*. It would be rather strange if this blessed God did not want to produce blessed people. A thoroughly happy God must want to make people happy. If only we Christians could begin to get back to the idea that our Lord came into this world, not to put people into evangelical straightjackets, not to put them under rigid systems that would squeeze the joy out of their existence, but to fill them full so they would go around the world and bring a message of *makarios*.

Of course, there are hindrances to blessing, to happiness, to contentment and fulfillment. Two words describe these hindrances: selfishness and sinfulness. Therefore, if a happy God is going to bring happy people to himself, do you know what he must do? He has to pinpoint the hindrances and eradicate them. There never was a thoroughly selfish man who was a truly happy man. A sinful man just cannot enjoy *makarios* living. Sin and selfishness stand in the way of our blessedness. Many Christians have the idea that sharing the gospel of Jesus Christ is telling sinners that they need to be convicted of their sin, telling selfish people to be unselfish. That isn't the gospel. That is simply pinpointing the hindrances between us and what God has in mind for us. We cannot combine blessedness with sinfulness and selfishness. If we want the blessedness, which is God's norm for society, sinfulness and selfishness have to go. This is what Jesus is saying with his repetition of the word, "Blessed. . . ."

In England a number of years ago we did a survey. We asked hundreds of young people, "What is your main ambition?" Most of them answered, "To be happy." They wanted happiness more than anything else. Some said they wanted to be married, that they expected to find happiness in that state. Most were not looking for money or fame. Having these things does not guarantee happiness. The great quest of the human soul, wherever you go throughout this wide world of ours, is basically, "How can I find *makarios*?" I'm excited and thrilled because as a Christian I have the answer to that basic life question. I represent a blessed God who wants men and women to have true happiness. As we begin to look at the Beatitudes in this chapter, we're going to discover what God has in mind for us. We're going to look in depth at just three of them, and we will see as we do that happiness is the product of character, and happiness is the promise of Christ.

Most people think that happiness is to be found in things. Actually, true happiness is to be found only in a right relationship with the God who alone gives reason and content to living. When we know him he brings joy through the things he has graciously given. But real happiness is not rooted in material things. It is independent of them. Possession of things is mere selfishness. It is a pseudo-happiness rooted in selfishness. God is the blessed God. From him comes blessedness. Here in the Sermon on the Mount Jesus goes on to point out that the happiness he's talking about is something not related to the temporal or the secular, the tangible or the material. Basically a spiritual experience, it is above these things.

Happiness Is a Product of Character

The first thing Jesus points out is that happiness is a product of a certain kind of character. Certain phrases in verses 3, 4, and 5 bear this out: "Blessed are the poor in spirit, ... they that mourn, ... " and "the meek." These three statements are a paradox to the modern secular mind. They fly right in the face of general opinion. "Blessed are the poor in spirit"? "Baloney!" says the secular man. "You have to get out there and do your own thing. You have to hack out your own little niche in the wilderness of the world." That's a rather simplified translation of society's philosophy.

With all due respect I would label that philosophy, "Baloney." The United States of America is filled with people who have lived by this erroneous philosophy, and they've hacked out their piece of the continent. They can stand on it with their feet firmly planted and their hands on their hips—and still they're miserable. Happiness does not come from centering one's life around oneself. No, blessedness comes only to the poor in spirit. You ask, "How can a person who's poor in spirit ever know happiness? If he's poverty-stricken in spirit, he's going to be unhappy because he's poor." Paradoxically enough, that isn't the way it works.

Look at it from God's perspective. When we recognize what we are, then we are ready to look at God realistically. When we know our need, then we're interested in what God gives. And what God gives is blessedness in the midst of what we are. Only a certain kind of character will admit his need.

What kind of character is "poor in spirit"? Such a person is realistic. He is thoroughly realistic about his situation in two particular areas: his own spiritual inability and his own spiritual inadequacy. He comes before his God and says, "God, you're the great God and I'm only a little piece of your creation. I want to tell you something. I have my own little world, and it's crumbling. I did my own thing, and it is not satisfying. I sought happiness everywhere people said it could be found, and I didn't find it. I have climbed to the end of the rainbow, and there was no pot of gold. Now what?" The Lord comes back to him and says, "I'll tell you what we'll do. Let's backtrack a bit, and let's look at you." Then the Lord points out to him his poverty. Outside of Christ we are poverty-stricken in spirit. Unless and until this is rectified we can never find fulfillment.

One of our main problems is that we do not recognize our spiritual impoverishment, our true spiritual condition. This is what makes happiness so elusive. Our basic spiritual problem is this: we are utterly poverty-stricken spiritually because we're completely devoid of spiritual ability. The spiritual poverty of human beings is beautifully described by Jesus in the word "cannot." "Jesus answered and said unto him [Nicodemus], 'Verily, verily, I say unto thee, Except a man be born again he *cannot* see the kingdom of God' " (John 3:3).

We are so spiritually inadequate and incapable that the Bible has to tell us what we can't do. Until we face up to our need, we'll never be interested in what God can do in our lives. Our interest will be in what we can do ourselves. And until we allow God to do in our lives what we cannot do for ourselves, we will never know *makarios*. Our root problem is simply refusing to admit: "I am spiritually incapable. I cannot enter the kingdom of heaven on my own. I can't."

This admission of weakness is one of the hardest things for a man to do. Because he has bought the philosophy that he can do anything if he puts his mind to it, he finds it impossible to say, "I can't." But let's face it. There's one thing we cannot do. We cannot enter the kingdom of heaven. That's a hard statement, but it's the truth. If we would only admit how poverty-stricken we are, then we might be interested in the blessedness that comes to poverty-stricken people who say, "Here I am, God. I can't enter the kingdom of heaven. Oh, God, do something for me." And he does. What does he do? *Makarios*.

Let's see what Jesus says to some religious leaders in another place. "Ye shall seek me, and shall not find me: and where I am, thither ye cannot come" (John 7:34). *Cannot come*. We say, "I can go any place I want. I can do anything I want to do. I can be anything I want to be. And if I go where I want to go, and be where I want to be, and do what I want to do, I'll be happy." Sounds great, but there's only one problem. There are some things we can't do, and there are some places we can't go, because of our spiritual inability and inadequacy. Let me give some scriptural examples of what I mean:

The realistic character is the one who says, "I am poor in spirit. There's so much I can't do." In John 15:4 Jesus said, "Abide in me, . . . As the branch cannot bear fruit of itself, except it abide in the vine; no more can ye, except ye abide in me." Note that word "cannot." What cannot a person do? We say, "I can produce if I want to. I could produce. I will produce." But God says, "No, you won't." We simply cannot. No way! There is no hope for us, says the Lord Jesus. We cannot produce what God expects a human being to produce apart from a relationship to Jesus Christ, no more than a branch can produce fruit when it has been severed from the tree. It isn't that the branch won't produce fruit. It is simply that the branch *cannot* produce fruit.

Paul tells us the same thing: "So then they that are in the flesh *cannot* please God" (Rom. 8:8). We say, "I'll please God when I want to. I don't want to right now, but I will when I'm ready. When I'm really happy. When I've got it made. When I've done what I want to, gone where I want to go, then I'll give God a chance, and I'll make God happy." God says, "No, you won't." We don't have what it takes in ourselves apart from God's grace. He must pour into us *makarios* before we can please him. We're never going to be interested in what God can pour into us until we realize how empty and incapable we really are. The divine principle, the controversial, paradoxical principle of happiness is totally the opposite of what man says. He says, "Get up there, boy. Build yourself up there, man. Be what you're going to be, man, and you'll be happy." God says, "Humble yourself. Admit what you are. Face the poverty of your own spiritual experience, and then I'll pour in *makarios*. Blessed are those who are realistic enough in character to admit their own spiritual inability."

To be poor in spirit also means to be realistic about our own spiritual *inadequacy*. Three Bible characters come to mind here: Jacob, Isaiah, and Gideon. They all had something in common. God wanted to bless them, to fill them, to use them. But he couldn't bless any of them, or fill them, or use them— until something very beautiful happened to each of them. They had to face their poverty of spirit. They not only had to admit their own spiritual inability, but also their own spiritual inadequacy.

What happened to Jacob? He fought God all night until God dislocated his hip, putting him flat on his back. Then he said, "Okay, God. I quit. I can't buck your system. I can't win. I can't be what I'm supposed to be without allowing you to be the God you intend to be. All right, I surrender." The Bible says, "And he [God] blessed him there" (Gen. 32:29). *Makarios*. The hardest thing for a person to do is to admit his poverty of spirit, but it's the only path to real happiness.

God was going to do fantastic things with Isaiah. He wanted him to be a beautiful prophet of the Old Testament, but something was in the way. Isaiah was all upset because the king had died. That's all he could think about—his loss. What did God do? God graciously gave Isaiah a vision of Himself high and lifted up. His train filled the temple. Isaiah saw the majestic heavenly temple and the throne. He saw the majestic, heavenly God. What did Isaiah say? "Woe is me! for I am undone; because I am a man of unclean lips . . . for mine eyes have seen the king . . . " (Isa. 6:5). In effect God was saying, "Amen. Great. You hear that, fellows?" And all the angels started clapping their wings! Isaiah had made it. God says, "Blessed are the poor in spirit, Isaiah. You're right. Woe is you. You are a man of unclean lips. You have seen the Lord. You're right. You don't have what it takes." *Makarios*. And God blessed him there.

God was going to do something with Gideon who was having trouble with his harvest. When it was all ready, his enemies would come at night and steal it. So Gideon decided to get ahead of them and harvest it before it was ripe. He hid behind the walls of his winepress to do his threshing. And what did God do? With a delightful touch of humor, God's angel says, "The Lord is with thee, thou mighty man of valor" (Judg. 6:12). Mighty man of valor? Right away Gideon began to make excuses. He wasn't the man for the job of conquering the enemy. But God said, "Go in this thy might, and thou shalt save Israel . . . " (Judg. 6:14). What kind of a man was Gideon? He was totally aware of his own spiritual inadequacy until God touched him and said, "Listen, mighty man of valor. I'm with you. This is thy might." *Makarios*. Now he could go out and *be* the mighty man of valor. Gideon finds contentment and fulfillment. If we ask him, "Gideon, what is happiness?" he would reply, "Happiness is just being realistic about yourself. It is admitting how poor in spirit you are and saying, 'Oh, God, what I need is you.' "

Not only is happiness a realistic characteristic, it is a repentant character as well. In Matthew 5 the Lord Jesus not only says, "Blessed are the poor in spirit." He goes on to say, "Blessed are they that mourn." It's part of the same package. We cannot be realistic about our own spiritual inability and our own spiritual inadequacy and leave it there. When you realize your own poverty of spirit, then you begin to understand the necessity for repentance. There is no happiness for the man who sees what is wrong with himself and does nothing about it. "Blessed are they that mourn" does not refer only to people who sit at a graveside. It does refer to them, but it refers to much more. Repentance comes deep in the soul of a man when he realizes all God has in mind for him and how little of it he has appropriated. When he begins to understand what God wants to do with, for, in, and through him, and he looks at what has not been achieved, his heart breaks. There is no *makarios* for the unrepentant. There is no blessedness for those who refuse to mourn. There is no fulfillment for those who reject the truth about themselves. They must come in brokenness, contrition, and confession before God.

Read Psalm 51 to see how David did it. He not only saw how utterly poverty-stricken he was, but he was also repentant, broken-hearted before God. So he confessed his sin.

Look at Job. Job had so much of everything, he didn't know what to do with it. Butter was scarce where he lived. Yet he had so much butter he washed his front doorstep with it (Job 29:6). That seems rather a strange custom—must have made the steps terribly slippery! But that's Job. He was the greatest, but he wasn't happy until he reached the point of Job 42:6, "I abhor myself, and repent in dust and ashes." Apparently it took forty-one chapters to bring Job to that point of repentance. And God says, "Amen. Job's made it. Blessed are the poor in spirit. Blessed are those that mourn. You've come to the point of realism. You've come to the point of repentance."

And God gave Job an oversized dose of *makarios*. Job was now happiness personified.

Happiness is the product of a character that is realistic and repentant before God. There is no *makarios* for the unrealistic and the unrepentant. Such people are fighting a losing battle and running a losing race.

Happiness is also the product of a character that is *responsive*. The third beatitude is "Blessed are the meek." Man says if you're going to be happy, you must go out into the big, hard, materialistic world and give it all you have. Man's idea of meekness is being a doormat, having spaghetti for a backbone.

Listen, meekness isn't synonymous with weakness! The word literally means "yieldedness." It is the natural product of a realistic character that is poor in spirit and a repentant character that mourns because of its poverty. It knows the only alternative open to it is responsive yielding to the blessed God. It isn't weakness. It's the opposite. It takes a certain moral strength to admit how desperately we need God and yield unreservedly to him. Why are there so many unhappy people in the world? Because they will not admit how poverty-stricken they are. They will not mourn for their sin, nor will they yield to God. That's why they are unhappy.

Jesus says, on the other hand, "Don't listen to all this stuff the world gives you. What I'm telling you is controversial—it's paradoxical. It runs counter to everything the world will tell you. But it's the truth. Will you admit your own inability, your own inadequacy? Will you mourn for your sin? Will you face your own situation and confess your sin? And then will you be responsive?"

Happiness is the product of character that is realistic, repentant, and responsive. Jesus said, "Blessed are the poor in spirit, . . . they that mourn, . . . the meek, . . . " He could have approached it from the opposite point of view: "Unblessed are the arrogant in spirit and self-sufficient. Singularly unblessed are those unrepentant, hard-necked, unyielding, uncommitted, unresponsive people. The unfulfilled are discontent and unhappy, completely devoid of joy." The blessed God says, "If only they knew what I have in store for them. If only they'd do it my way." Happiness is the product of character.

Happiness Is . . . the Promise of Christ

Notice three things here concerning the promise of Christ. First, the authority of his statements. The Lord Jesus didn't just sit there apologetically on the Mount and say, "Now, fellows, listen. Blessed are the poor in spirit, I think. Blessed are they that mourn, so I understand. Blessed are the meek, so I've been told. You see, fellows, I don't know how it works, but I think the poor in spirit are blessed because I think God might give them a little piece of the kingdom. I'm not sure, but I think so. And I think those who mourn are blessed because I think God will comfort them. You know, he's like that. . . . " Jesus just did not talk that way.

Notice the calm certainty of his statements: "Blessed are the poor . . . for they *shall* . . . "; "Blessed are they that mourn, for they *shall* . . . "; "Blessed are the meek, for they *shall*. . . . " He declared it unequivocally. I use the repetitive to emphasize this point: Blessing is what God has for his people. The authority of Jesus is rooted in the authoritative God who says, "This is the way it is." To find happiness we merely accept.

Secondly, I must understand the availability of his blessings. What is the blessing available for the poor in spirit? The kingdom of heaven. What is the blessing for those who mourn? Comfort. For those who are meek? They shall inherit the earth.

What is God saying here? He is saying that if a person will admit his inadequacy, his inability in the spiritual realm, if he will confess it and repent of it, and yield to God, God will give him the kingdom. He will have unbelievable riches in exchange for unbearable poverty.

Then Jesus added: "If a man will repent, and come in brokenness and contrition before me, he will be comforted and forgiven." The word comforted here in the Greek is the one closely related to the name given the Holy Spirit—the Comforter. It doesn't mean just someone coming along and patting you on the head, mopping your fevered brow. It means "one called alongside to help, one called alongside to impart strength." This is entering the kingdom and enjoying its riches, appropriating the Comforter and knowing his strength.

Jesus also says, "Blessed are the meek, for they shall inherit the earth." Perhaps a better translation is: "They shall inherit the land." Remember how the Israelites went into the new land and possessed it? After routing their enemies, they set their feet firmly on what God had given them and thoroughly enjoyed it. Oh, blessed are the meek. They're going to rout their enemies; they're going to stand firm in all that God has formed for them; they're going to possess their possessions.

Let's look one final time at the word, *makarios*. The *makarios* is all the riches of the kingdom imparted to poverty-stricken people. It is all the strength of the Comforter given to broken people. It is nothing less than the possession of all our possessions and the routing of all our enemies. All we have to do is come in yieldedness to God. Where then does the happiness come from? It comes through the acceptance of what Jesus offers. Outside of Christ, man must say, "I am singularly unblessed. Now I know why. I accept the authority of your statements. I believe in the availability of your blessings, and I accept all that you have in mind for me. I come humbly, contritely, broken in spirit. I come to you in faith." When a man can say this, he is on the way to blessing, fulfillment, contentment, and happiness. This shouldn't surprise us, because we have a blesssed God! Let's live *makariosly*.

3

The Christian

and More Happiness

In this chapter we are continuing to look at happiness as a product of character. There are three aspects of the matter I'd like you to note: ambition, attitude, and action. In Matthew 5:6 Jesus talks about those who "hunger and thirst after righteousness." Hungering and thirsting is a rather descriptive term for *ambition*. God requires a certain kind of character in those who would follow him. They are to be ambitious, but theirs is to be an ambition based on that which is right. This commitment to the right is the basis of the blessing of God in my life. The full flow of his blessing comes from his righteousness lived out in me.

The next beatitude (Matt. 5:7) calls for a certain *attitude* in the child of God: "Blessed are the merciful, for they shall obtain mercy." The word "merciful" might better be translated "kind." If my ambition is based on that which is right and my attitude on that which is kind, then I will begin to see God producing in me the full flow of his blessing.

If God's intention were simply to take Christians to heaven, he would lead them to a decision and then whisk them off. But that is not his plan. His intention is to make Christians and leave them on earth that they might be a channel for change in society. The people who create change are those who know the blessing of God, who have their attitudes right.

The third beatitude calls for a certain *action,* action based on truth. Jesus says, "Blessed are the pure in heart: for they shall see God" (Matt. 5:8). The Greek word for pure means literally to be free from alloy, to be free from impurity. When you read the word pure in this context in Scripture, it means singleness of mind and purpose. Is our world today characterized by action? Definitely yes. But are the actions seen in our world today absolutely based on integrity, sincerity, and truthfulness? Emphatically no. That is the degree to which our society needs the church of Jesus Christ. The beautiful thing about being a Christian and a member of the church of Jesus Christ is this: We are called to be totally different and distinctive. As we are, the blessing of God comes upon our lives.

One of the mistakes many Christians make today is this. They want to be just like the world and also blessed of God. This is impossible. We can be just like the society around us, with ambition like theirs, an attitude like theirs, and involved in activities like theirs—but forget the *makarios* in that case. On the other hand, we can major on the *makarios.* We can say, "God, nothing really matters to me more than your blessing upon my life." In that case, our activities are going to change from those of the world around us. We're going to be God's men and women in society, receiving his blessing. That is the promise of Christ.

Ambition

Ambition is normal. A person without ambition, lacking motivation, has a problem (besides being lazy!). Such a person needs to discover he has worth. A human being can never be worthless, for he is divinely created. God created him to fulfill a certain function. His overriding ambition at least ought to be to find out why God made him.

It is proper to have ambition—it is an integral part of our personhood. It is an integral part of being what God intended human beings to be. But that ambition may be perverted. There are some examples from the Scriptures that show us that perversion of ambition is quite possible.

Look with me at Lucifer, son of the morning, one of God's

most glorious creations, a masterpiece. He was supremely beautiful and absolutely magnificent. What was his driving ambition? Isaiah records it for us: "For thou [Lucifer] hast said in thine heart, I will ascend into heaven, I will exalt my throne above the stars of God: I will sit also upon the mount of the congregation . . . I will ascend above the heights of the clouds; I will be like the Most High" (Isa. 14:13,14). The driving ambition of Lucifer's angelic soul was to be like God! He was power-hungry. Anyone who is hungry for power for its own sake is a victim of perverted ambition. But you will find these power-hungry people in the big arena of national politics, or in the small arena of the local church. You will find them everywhere—bullies in the school, teachers behind the desks. In the business world this craze for power runs rampant.

This is a perversion of ambition which God totally rejects. When Lucifer made his grab for power, how did God react? Isaiah gives us his reply to Lucifer's boast: "Yet thou shalt be brought down . . . " (14:15).

In the parable of the rich fool recorded in Luke 12, Jesus spoke of a certain rich man who had done well in business. One day he thought to himself, "What shall I do, because I have nowhere to store my crops?" (12:17, rsv). So he decided to pull down his old barns and build larger ones. That sounds like good business practice. What's wrong with that ambition? Nothing at all. If God has given a businessman intelligence and ability, then God is going to bless him. He is going to say, "Go right ahead, friend, because every penny you make is mine. The more you make for me the more pleased I'll be."

Make no mistake about it. God is going to give some people the ability to gain wealth, and others will not have so much of this ability. This is what creates the difficulty. Wealth always brings problems along with it. Those who have money, have problems knowing what to do with it. And those who do not have money encounter problems trying to get it.

What did the man in the parable do? He tore down his old barns and built larger ones, saying to his soul in the process, "Soul, you have ample goods laid up for many years; take your ease, eat, drink, be merry" (Luke 12:19, rsv). His goal was to make as big a pile as possible so he could retire and enjoy himself. His problem was not power-hunger—it was pleasure-hunger. Hungering and thirsting after fun, he was absolutely eaten up with the desire to have a good time. It's very interesting to note God's commentary on this kind of ambition. God used one word to describe him: "Fool!" (Luke 12:20). Need I say more? God has a succinct way of expressing himself, doesn't he? When a man's ambition is perverted to power-hunger, God brings him down. And when a man's ambition is simply devoted to pleasure-seeking, God calls him a fool and brings him down.

A man called Nebuchadnezzar is another example of perverted ambition. Daniel tells us about him. He was doing pretty well, but he was hungry for more fame. He loved the adulation of the crowds, but he had a problem. Daniel had just counseled him: "Wherefore, O king, let my counsel be acceptable unto thee, and break off thy sins by righteousness, and thine iniquities by showing mercy to the poor . . ." (4:27). Daniel sounds just like Jesus here, doesn't he, talking about righteousness and mercy? But what was the king's reply? "Is not this great Babylon, that I have built for the house of the kingdom by the might of my power, and for the honor of my majesty?" (4:30). Doesn't sound very humble, does he? "I'm going to make absolutely certain that everyone around here knows about Nebuchadnezzar." But God says, "No, you won't." Daniel 4:31,32 records it: "O king Nebuchadnezzar, to thee it is spoken; The kingdom is departed from thee. And they shall drive thee from men, and thy dwelling shall be with the beasts of the field: they shall make thee to eat grass as oxen, and seven times shall pass over thee, until thou know that the Most High ruleth in the kingdom of men, and giveth it to whomsoever he will." God has a striking way of expressing himself, doesn't he, when people's ambitions are perverted?

Do you know what Jesus said? Ambition is all right. You must hunger and thirst, but make absolutely certain that your ambition is not perverted. "Blessed are they which do hunger and thirst after righteousness: for they shall be filled" (Matt. 5:6). Having been warned that ambition can be perverted, we must notice exactly what Jesus said: "Ambition must be directed." If we are to be God's men and women in a sick society, what should be our overriding ambition? It should not be hunger for power, fun, or fame. It should be to *possess* righteousness, then to *practice* righteousness, and finally to *promote* righteousness. Righteousness is to be my overwhelming ambition if I'm to be God's man on earth. I'm afraid this is not the case in all too many instances in the church. Our ambitions are basically directed in the areas of those perverted ambitions that God has categorically condemned and rebuked in the Scriptures.

"Blessed are they which do hunger and thirst after righteousness. . . ." What does it mean, first of all, to have an ambition to possess righteousness? In Philippians 3:6 Paul gives us an answer. He says that he was ". . . touching the righteousness which is in the law, blameless." Paul had quite a pedigree, as he reminds us in this chapter. But he discovered he could not establish his own righteousness, so he came to God and said, "God, I've been trying to establish my own righteousness. All I am is self-righteous. Now I understand. Self-righteousness won't do because I can never establish my own. Please forgive me and impart to me the righteousness of Jesus Christ." What does he mean? He means he saw himself as a person who needed the grace, mercy, and forgiveness of God. When he accepted Jesus Christ as his Savior, the righteousness of Christ was reckoned to him. Now he says, "My overriding ambition when I began to understand myself was to possess righteousness."

What happens when people are in a crisis situation—aboard a hijacked airliner, a sinking ship, a runaway train? Suddenly the petty concerns of everyday life are seen in their true perspective, and the important issues become important once again. When a person believes he has forty-two more *minutes* to live, he is a different person than the one who assumes he has forty-two *years* to live. Suddenly his interests and ambitions change. He becames realistic, just as the apostle Paul become realistic in assessing his life. He had suddenly discovered that all his earthly ambitions were really secondary, that the supreme ambition of any sane person ought to be to get right with God. Can you imagine a person not making this priority number one? When my back is to the wall I realize that my relationship to God is the most important concern I have.

When I was about twenty-five years of age, I was interviewed for a beautiful job in a bank. The official who conducted the interview (who later became my boss) asked me, "What are your ambitions?" The Lord was dealing with my life very definitely at that time, and I replied, "Sir, my ambitions are quite simply to serve God." He almost swallowed his mustache. At the end of the interview he shook hands with me and said, "Young man, it has been refreshing to meet someone who knows what he believes and why he believes it. I want you to work for me."

Many people who profess to be God's men fall short of this position in a job situation, because they know the employer is not necessarily looking for a man whose ambition is to practice righteousness. They decide to be God's man in the church, but not on the job. When this happens what do we find in the business world? Everyone is squeezed into a pale gray anemic mold. No one stands out as God's man.

Not only are we to be hungry to possess righteousness, and to practice it, but we are also to promote righteousness. "Righteousness exalteth a nation" (Prov. 14:34). We know that. This verse is often quoted. There isn't any such thing as a Christian nation. We can have "In God we trust" on our coins, but that doesn't make us a Christian nation. We can have a church on every corner, but that doesn't make ours a Christian nation. That which exalts a nation in the sight of God is righteousness *possessed* by individuals, *practiced* by society, and *promoted* by people who have the voice.

Let's speak out for righteousness. If we do, we'll encounter opposition. A worker who says to his employer, "I'm terribly sorry, sir. I can't do what you're asking because it's against my Christian principles. I can't take the path of least resistance because it would mean letting the expedient dictate my actions rather than my conscience. My ambition, my overwhelming hunger and thirst is to do that which is right. What you're asking me to do is the most profitable but also the most unethical. Therefore, I cannot do it." What would the boss's reaction be? If your ambition is channeled in the right direction, that will not be your main concern. Your main concern will be to please God. Society says that right must *not* be the first priority. Rather, the easy way, the expedient action is more important than righteousness. Even some of our country's leaders are saying that the ends justify any means. We cannot expect God to exalt a nation that has allowed its moral, ethical, and spiritual principles to erode so far they almost no longer exist. The church of Jesus Christ has to be hungry, ambitious for that which is right. It starts with us, you and me, as individuals, and spreads out like ripples in a pond.

Attitude

A society that is not only based on perverted ambition, but also has a perverted attitude, has to have problems. What a marvelous thing it is to be a Christian in a society with problems, knowing that you are God's means of rectifying the problems. Jesus said, "Blessed are the merciful: for they shall obtain mercy" (Matt. 5:7). A Christian is merciful; he is kind. A practicing Christian goes the extra mile and turns the other cheek. Why? Because his God is rich in mercy. If there were no other call given in Scripture, I would expect Christians to be merciful people for this very simple reason: Our God is a merciful God. Grace is God giving us what we don't deserve. Mercy is God withholding from us what we *do* deserve. Merciful kindness is seeing someone reap the results of his rash actions, and being heartbroken over their pain. It's the opposite of the one who gloats over the misfortunes of others.

The church of Jesus Christ is supposed to be full of kind people, reproduced by a merciful God. Are you and I known as kind people? Or are we mainly interested in our own small world, our own concerns, our own tiny circle? A kind person will be characterized by concern more for others than for himself. He will stand out from the crowd because of his concern. This world does not like different people. But the world needs the kindness you and I can bring because our roots are in our merciful God.

Action

In Matthew 5:8 Jesus says, "Blessed are the pure in heart: for they shall see God." Purity speaks of unmixed sincerity and integrity in action. Action springs from motivation, and our actions must always be evaluated in the light of that which motivates them. Ananias and Sapphira did what appeared to be a magnificent thing. They sold some land and took part of the money to give to the church. This was a voluntary, benevolent, philanthropic, and spiritual action on their part. They didn't have to do it. What was wrong then? Why did God condemn them? It was because of their impure motive. They wore the façade of total dedication—conveying to their fellow church members the impression that they were giving all the money they had received. In reality, however, they were holding back part of the money. The Living Bible points out: "There was a man named Ananias (with his wife Sapphira) who sold some property, and brought only part of the money, claiming it was the full price. (His wife had agreed to this deception)" (Acts 5:1,2). Their action was good, but their motivation was impure.

One of the sad things happening in our society today is this: We evaluate people by external standards, without any knowledge of their motivations. In this sixth beatitude Jesus was saying in effect, "Your actions will be blessed when they are more than just actions—when they are motivated by that which is right and true. When you act on the basis of integrity, when there is no insincerity in you, then you are 'pure in heart.' " I know this kind of living is next to impossible in the contemporary world, but it is the life style Jesus demands— and gives us the strength to perform. He knows our hearts, and while people around us can accuse us of all kinds of false motivations (because they do not know our hearts, and would condemn us even if they did), he is at our side encouraging us along the way. In Psalm 51 David says, "Behold, thou desirest truth in the inward parts . . ." (v. 6). This is the way the candidate for God's blessing must pray. He must be transparent and open before God and man. This is the path to *makarios* living.

One final thought. Happiness is not only the product of character, it is the promise of Christ. What does he promise? "... they shall be filled." The Bible teaches that the Christian life is a full life. In Colossians Paul says, "And ye are *complete* in him ..." (2:10). This expression means literally "filled full." Of what? The fullness of Christ, the fullness of the very Godhead. And out of our fullness will flow rivers of living water to the dry and barren world around us. Not only does he promise spiritual fullness, but he also promises us natural kindness, flowing from the mercy of God himself. If you want kindness, how do you get it? By showing kindness.

A word of warning. These behavior patterns I have been discussing do not *earn* salvation. They are the *evidence* of salvation. Only Christians are enabled by the risen Christ to live life *makariosly.*

4

The Christian

and Peacemaking

We have progressed in our thinking to beatitudes 7 and 8: "Blessed are the peacemakers: for they shall be called the children of God" and "Blessed are they which are persecuted for righteousness' sake: for theirs is the kingdom of heaven" (Matt. 5:9,10). No passage in the whole Bible speaks more succinctly, more powerfully, more challengingly than the Sermon on the Mount. In it Jesus is dealing with the question of how a Christian should behave. Whatever one's interpretation of this passage might be, it unquestionably enunciates divine principles of behavior. These principles are God's requirements for his children. To that end he equips us through the indwelling presence of the Holy Spirit to live our lives after this fashion.

So far we have seen that happiness is a product of character: "Blessed are the poor in spirit, . . . they that mourn, . . . the meek, . . . they which do hunger and thirst after right-eousness, . . . the merciful, . . . the pure in heart." Happiness is a product of character such as this, but it is also the promise of Christ. What blessings there are for the person who will put himself in the place of blessing, being poor in spirit before God, claiming the promise of Christ.

Happiness is the product of a character that pursues peace. It is also the product of a character that persists under persecution. These are the areas of life with which we are dealing in this chapter.

At first glance, there seems to be a conflict here. How can we talk about peace and persecution in the same breath? How can a Christian know the same kind of happiness in peace as he does in persecution? We usually think of peace as the absence of something like persecution. "If I'm at peace, there won't be persecution, and if there's persecution, there won't be peace." Not so. Our understanding of peace usually assumes that peace is the absence of hostility. Again not so. Look at the international situation. The East and the West have been co-existing under what might be called a very uneasy peace for many years. A cold war is certainly not synonymous with peace. In the sense that we're not shooting at one another, we're at peace. But it's a shaky truce at best—not peace.

We don't know from one day to the next how the Arabs and the Israelis will handle their differences. Hot war could erupt at the slightest provocation. This is not peace. When God talks about peace he doesn't mean merely the absence of overt hostility. He is dealing with the ability to triumph over hostility and know a quality of divine life in the midst of it. It is possible to know peace when all around you is war. It takes someone in whom the Spirit of God is working to be at peace when everything is going wrong. On that basis we are not dealing with a contradiction when we say that blessedness is the product of character that pursues peace and yet persists under persecution. The two can live together.

Let's look first of all at the character that pursues peace. There are four areas of thought I'd like you to note: the passion for peace, the price of peace, the pursuit of peace, and the prize of peace.

The Passion for Peace

What do I mean by the passion for peace? I believe a real impact will be made on society through the life of one who passionately desires peace. Peace must be something he really longs to see and to produce in his own life. Many Christians lack this heartfelt desire for peace. They prefer to settle for mutual coexistence, a cold war. This kind of false peace is not the true peace of which God speaks. God wants people who have a passion for peace, who will verbalize their faith. One of the basic characteristics of Christian character in a non-Christian world is to be a peacemaker with a desire to see other people discover that peace.

In 2 Corinthians 5:20 Paul indicates that our passion for peace will be primarily a passion for spiritual peace: "Now then we are ambassadors for Christ, as though God did beseech you by us: we pray you in Christ's stead, be ye reconciled to God." What is Paul praying? He is sharing a passionate desire for men and women to discover spiritual peace. Paul is a striking example of what I mean by a person who has a passion for peace. Jesus said, "Blessed are the peacemakers." It takes a special kind of dedication to produce a man or woman who is just burning with a passion for men or women to be reconciled to God. Blessed are the peacemakers who are in the world making peace between God and man, and between man and God.

Not only are we to have a passion for spiritual peace, we are to have a passion for social peace as well. Paul spells it out for us in Romans 12:17,18: "Recompence to no man evil for evil. Provide things honest in the sight of all men. If it be possible, as much as lieth in you, live peaceably with all men." There in verse 18 are two tremendously important clauses. They take this concept out of the realm of the idealistic and bring it down into the realm of the realistic where we all live. Paul doesn't say bluntly, "Live peaceably with all men." There's no way you can live peaceably with some people. No matter what you do, they will not accept you. But Paul isn't talking idealistically here; he is speaking realistically. He says, "*If it be possible, as much as lieth in you*, live peaceably with all men." What is our typical reaction when someone wrongs us or takes advantage of us? Retaliation! It really isn't surprising that our hostile world discounts our Christianity. So many times our attitudes and our behavior are totally identical to theirs.

Let's bring it even closer home. I would suggest that this passion for peace would make a vital difference in many marriages. This lack of peace is one of the chronic problems in American society today—marriages severed by warfare rather than drawn together by mutual love.

What would happen in industry if the overriding desire was for peace? What if the Christian in industry would really put this principle of peacemaking into practice?

This command implies a passion for personal peace as well. In Matthew 5:24 (later in his Sermon on the Mount) Jesus said, "Leave there thy gift before the altar, and go thy way; first be reconciled to thy brother, and then come and offer thy gift." Often we Christians go to a worship service with unprepared hearts. We bring both our gift and our resentment. As Christians we are responsible for our own attitudes. If I have anything against a brother Christian, or if he has anything against me, that should be confessed and the slate cleared before I come before God in worship. I am not responsible for the attitude of the other person, but I am responsible to do all I can by confession and a desire for peace, to make sure nothing separating me from another person will come between me and my God.

The Price of Peace

"Having made peace through the blood of his cross, by him to reconcile all things unto himself; by him, I say, whether they be things in earth, or things in heaven" (Col. 1:20). Paul is speaking here of the same kind of peacemaking that Jesus was talking about in the Sermon on the Mount. How did Jesus make peace? Through the blood of his cross. The price of the spiritual peace between God and man, the cost of reconciliation, was the blood of the cross. This is the value God has placed upon peace—the blood of his own Son! If I do not have a passion for peace and a deep-seated desire to see others come under the blanket of that reconciliation, am I trampling underfoot that precious blood shed to pay for that peace?

The price of peace is more than blood shed, it is also barriers broken down. Often we fail to have peace with other people simply because we feel threatened by them. Our natural reaction when we are threatened is to build defenses, barriers between ourselves and the source of the threat. Once we have defenses, we naturally assume a defensive attitude.

If there are barriers between me and another person, I don't solve the problem by attacking his defenses. I approach it by tearing down my own defenses. I make myself vulnerable. One of the reasons peace is not restored in many relationships is simply this: We want others to lower their defenses before we do anything about ours. *If I lower my guard*, we reason, *he'll get me.* This is the crux of the matter. This is the heart of the peacemaker who is willing to pay the price for peace.

If I'm going to build a bridge between myself and another person, I have to start on my side. Have you ever seen a bridge built? The builders start with a solid structure on each side of the body of water they want to span. Then a thin little cable is sent across, securely fastened at one side, and secured at the other. That is the basis for the bridge—a thin little cable starting from one side but eventually connected at both ends. That's the way it is with peacemaking. It must start with me. That is what Jesus was calling for when he said, "Blessed are the peacemakers. . . ."

When does peace begin to be made? When blood is shed, when barriers are broken down. Why don't people live in peace? Because each one is waiting for the other to bring the cable. And no bridge is ever made. Pay the price. Shed the blood. Break the barriers. Build the bridges. This is the price of peace.

The Pursuit of Peace

In 1 Peter 3:10,11 (RSV) the apostle writes, "He that would love life and see good days, let him keep his tongue away from evil and his lips from speaking guile; let him turn away from evil and do right; *let him seek peace and pursue it*" (italics mine). The King James Version uses the word, "ensue," which is the same word translated "persecute" in Matthew 5. It means to relentlessly hunt a thing down. Saul of Tarsus was a persecutor. Indeed, he was on his way to Damascus to do some serious hunting when he met the Master. This is the way we are to pursue peace. In the vernacular we would probably say, "Kill them with kindness."

Let me point out and lay to rest some misconceptions about the pursuit of peace. No Christian is given the right to be at peace with evil. There is no such thing in the divine economy as "peace at any price." If God would have been satisfied with peace at any price, he would have found a cheaper price than the blood of the cross. He would have come to terms with Satan and sin. We are to pursue peace—but never by settling for evil or error.

One of the tragedies in the church today is the existence of "peace" at the expense of truth. We can never build peace by accepting evil. We can never build peace by condoning error.

This leads us into the matter of church discipline. There are times when discipline must be exercised and error must be isolated to view. Years ago my idea of a peacemaker was a skinny, anemic little guy who allowed people to trample all over him. Frankly, that's not my way! But to be a peacemaker in the biblical sense is anything but my impression. It's a rough, challenging occupation. We cannot have a healthy church if our idea of church discipline is "peace at any price." Problems in the church must be dealt with in love, but with firmness.

The fruit of the Spirit is love, joy, and peace (among other characteristics). How do I pursue peace? In the enabling power of the Holy Spirit. Don't think it's an automatic process, however. Just because the Spirit is in me does not mean I'm automatically a peacemaker. It simply means that now I'm free to *pursue* peace. Now I'm free to do something about this indwelling spiritual conviction out in the world where I as a Christian must make a difference.

The Prize of Peace

The blessings of God are contentment, joy, happiness, all deep-rooted in a right relationship to God. These are the ingredients of the peacemaker's life. This *makarios* life is the prize of peace. A sense of fulfillment that overflows the spirit is the prize of peace. Notice the last part of this beatitude: "for they shall be called the children of God" (Matt. 5:9). Not *become* children of God—that happens when we accept Christ. We become children of God by receiving Jesus Christ.

No, to be *called* children of God means to become known as a child of God because of our peacemaking attitude. It means nothing less than the recognition of a hostile world. This leads us right back to the subject of the earlier part of this chapter. Happiness is not only the product of a character that pursues peace. It is also the product of a character that persists under persecution. Jesus put it in perspective for us: "Think not that I am come to send peace on earth: I came not to send peace, but a sword" (Matt. 10:34). This verse links the two together—peace and persecution. Remember the adoration that surrounded the manger at the birth of Christ—and the anger that came down from Herod just a short time later? Think of the adulation Christ received on Palm Sunday—and the hatred that descended on him later that same week. The kind of peace that Jesus came to bring—some people welcome it, but others are antagonistic toward him and the reconciliation he offers.

The same kind of reception awaits you and me as Christians as we go out into the arena of the world. If we go out where the action is, if we get involved in the battle, we will discover that our peace will lead us into persecution. Some husbands, and some wives, will meet persecution when they live Christ-controlled lives in their homes. Some workers will encounter persecution on the job because of their outspoken faith.

Let me close with this final thought. We have all heard of the great Tribulation, and a battle has been raging for generations as to what this event really means and when it is going to take place. In all honesty I must say that much of the interest in the subject of the Tribulation appears to stem from a desire to make sure we will not go through it! This hardly seems to be the attitude that leads to blessing according to our Lord's teaching. We should not be concentrating on avoiding pressure but rather ensuring that we live "makariosly" under pressure.

What about the persecution our Christian brothers and sisters behind the iron curtain have already endured? I would say theirs has been the deepest of tribulation experiences. I have a friend in Czechoslovakia who speaks five languages fluently, including Japanese. He had to give up his business because he would not follow the communist party line when his country was taken over. He now works as a hotel porter. Another friend was a doctor of law. After the communist takeover he became a church secretary.

We can expect tribulation to come upon those who choose to stand firm for Christ—even ourselves. The beatitude says, "Blessed are ye, *when* men shall revile you, and persecute you . . ." (Matt. 5:11). Notice, it is *when* not if. Persecution is coming upon us, make no mistake on that score. Our identification with Christ automatically means alienation from Satan. Our identification with truth automatically means alienation from lies. And alienation is a close relative of persecution.

When does the blessing come? When I persist under persecution. Why are so few Christians blessed—and so many singularly unblessed? The moment persecution comes, they quit under its pressure. May that never be said of you and me!

5

The Christian
As the Salt of the Earth

Having outlined the principles and qualities that make Christians distinctive, the Lord Jesus now goes on to give a striking picture of what it really means to behave as a Christian:

> Ye are the salt of the earth: but if the salt have lost his savor, wherewith shall it be salted? it is thenceforth good for nothing, but to be cast out, and to be trodden under foot of men (Matt. 5:13).

Here Jesus provides a powerful illustration of the impact and impression Christians should be making on the society in which they live.

The word "earth" here refers to our little piece of geography, our little sphere of influence. We are responsible to "live out" our Christianity where God has placed us, to behave ourselves distinctively as Christians where we are. The size of our influence is not our concern. The fact of our influence is our concern. Christ said, "Ye *are* the salt. . . . " The question is not whether we are salt or not—the question is whether we are *functioning* as salt, or not functioning. In this chapter we are going to be looking at three aspects of that question: the status of being salt, the significance of being salt, and the seriousness of being salt.

The Status of Being Salt

What does it mean to be salt? Jesus isn't asking for volunteers here. He is saying, "Gentlemen, whether you want to be or not, you are salt." This means that God has a plan for each one of us, a function for each of us to fulfill. Each of us is to function as salt in the little piece of geography to which he has called us: our neighborhood, the office, or wherever we are. Now we know that we are to make an impact upon that area of influence where God has placed us. How can any Christian be bored or blasé when he realizes this truth? How can we be less than excited and exhilarated by this call to the "normal Christian life"?

An important aspect of this whole concept of being salt is that the world around us requires that Christians be salt. Just because we Christians are forgiven and on our way to heaven, does not mean that's all there is! Our role isn't to sit back and wait for the bus to pick us up. God knows how critically important we are to our world. If we are to fulfill our God-given role as salt, we can never settle down to a *mundane* existence. Salt is desperately needed. Let me illustrate.

When I was in the Marines, we used to go on speed marches. On a speed march you simply run all the way. When you come to a hill, you run twice as fast! All we had to eat on those marches was salt, actual chunks of it. Perspiration would blind us, but as long as we had the salt, we could go on, but without it we could not survive.

In the Middle East, salt is one of the most precious commodities available. Life functions require salt. It is the very sustenance of life itself, and in Jesus' day as now, salt was vital and pivotal in the life style of the people.

What an exciting concept! You and I as Christians are vital to the world around us. We can say, "O God, if this little piece of geography is to survive as You intended, if the people in it are to survive, it actually needs me as its salt." That gives Christianity a totally new dimension. The saltiness of the Christian is imperative for survival.

Salt is also distinctive in nature. Christians are to stand out from the crowd. They are to be different in their approach to life. Not only should our life style be distinctive, we should also serve as the world's "early warning system." When the world around us seems bent on its own destruction, or indifferent to its own danger, we Christians are to stand up and be counted, not just for the sake of being different—but to be the "salt" that preserves and purifies. We march to a different drummer; we live by a different set of principles. The world around us must know this. The little section of society in which we circulate takes a different view of life than we do. There are two basic views: God's view and man's view. We represent God, and the world desperately needs his view.

Not only is salt imperative for survival and distinctive in nature, it is also abrasive in character. Let me illustrate what I mean from the Bible.

A certain little town is described in Judges 18:

> Then the five men spies departed, and came to Laish, and saw the people that were therein, how they dwelt careless, after the manner of the Zidonians, quiet and secure; and there was no magistrate . . . (v.7).

Everyone in Laish was living comfortably, lacking nothing and possessing wealth. In the face of an approaching enemy, they remained unconcerned. They who were living comfortably perished comfortably! If only there had been one man who had stood to his feet and shouted, "Fools! Wake up!" The people would have been upset at one who rocked the boat this way. They might have called him an oddball. But he might have saved their lives.

This is the kind of abrasive character we Christians are to have. We are to confront people around us with the truth in total contrast to the lies that are lulling them to sleep. That's what it means to be a Christian: abrasive, distinctive, imperative. This is the status of being salt.

The Significance of Being Salt

What did Jesus' statement concerning the Christian's responsibility to be salt mean to his immediate hearers—the fishermen of Galilee? Those fishermen knew immediately what he was talking about. For them, salt was not something in a shiny silver shaker on the dinner table. It was a preservative, vital to their way of life. Once they caught a fish, they had to get it to market. The only way to get it there in marketable condition was to salt it down, pack it between layers of salt so that they could carry it with them down to the market in Jerusalem, where it could be sold as fresh as when they caught it. Salt arrested corruption; it kept fish fresh and edible.

We Christians today are to arrest the corruption in our society. Unfortunately, many Christians do not even know what is going on in the world around them; they are unaware of the terrible conditions that exist unchecked. This is one of the reasons, I believe, why we are not making a difference in the world around us.

On the contrary, Paul was aware of his world when he wrote, "For the preaching of the cross is to them that perish foolishness; but unto us which are saved it is the power of God" (1 Cor. 1:18). What has that to do with being salt? "Perishing" describes the condition of society today very aptly. Theirs is a perishing condition. The same word used in the original Greek for "perishing" is also used for "lost." Jesus used the latter word in describing the prodigal son and the lost coin, as well as the lost sheep, in his parables. People around us are in a lost condition, the victims of a disease known as sin. It is the element that causes their lostness and their corruption. Paul recognized it, and Jesus called for his followers to be the salt that would halt that condition. If the corruption is not arrested, those who are now in the process of perishing will one day finally, ultimately, and irrevocably perish for all eternity. We Christians are placed in the midst of this perishing, corrupt society to do what we can to halt the corruption, to stem the tide of godlessness all around us.

There are many ways for us to do this. Some feel it can be done through local government. Others think national politics can make the difference. Still others feel that by being involved in helping agencies of one kind or another, they can turn the tide. But what is the basic way to do it? We must get at the root of corruption in the individual. His condition must be changed. Instead of being in the process of perishing, he must be saved. The problem is basically spiritual, even though it has social implications and ramifications. That is why the Christian's main concern as salt is to arrest the corruption in society, by being the instrument to bring individuals in society to a knowledge of Christ and an experience of salvation. You and I are the means God can use to arrest the corruption in the world around us. Are we functioning as salt?

Salt has another meaning in the Scriptures. Even today in the Middle East business agreements and other arrangements are sealed with salt. Numbers 18:19 gives us the background of this usage: "All the heave offerings of the holy things, which the children of Israel offer unto the Lord, have I given thee, and thy sons and thy daughters with thee, by a statute for ever: it is a covenant of salt for ever before the Lord unto thee and to thy seed with thee." This "covenant of salt" is a symbolic thing which had real meaning for those who heard Jesus speaking on the mount. What is the meaning of salt in this context? It is a means of introducing the covenant between God and man. As we share our experience with Christ we are passing along this covenant of salt, this promise of truth. Men can "bite into" our experience to test its reality, allowing us the tremendous privilege of being salt to our society. We attest to the world which desperately needs our message that God is prepared to make a new covenant through the blood of his Son. In 2 Corinthians 3:6 Paul tells us God " . . . has qualified us to be ministers of a new covenant, not in a written code but in the Spirit; for the written code kills, but the Spirit gives life" (RSV).

Are you and I as Christians truly functioning as salt? Are many people around us coming to grips with the fact that it is possible for God and man to be reconciled through the blood of his cross? Do they know it is possible for lostness, corruption, and alienation to be done away with because we are salt? That's what it means to be salt.

This brings us to a third significance of salt. In the Old Testament we are told that it was a military practice in destroying the enemy to sow his city with salt: "And Abimelech fought against the city all that day; and he took the city, and slew the people that was therein, and beat down the city, and sowed it with salt" (Judg. 9:45). This was done so that nothing would ever grow in the area again. It was totally and utterly destroyed. This is the way a Christian should function. His life, his testimony, his very presence should be a positive witness for Christ, but it should be a negative condemnation to the person who refuses to believe.

Writing to the Corinthians, Paul makes this point: "For we are unto God a sweet savor of Christ, in them that are saved, and in them that perish: to the one we are the savor of death unto death; and to the other the savor of life unto life" (2 Cor. 2:15,16). I believe this is the reason many Christians fall by the wayside. They want to live comfortably like the people of Laish. They don't want to upset or perturb anyone. But some people need to be upset and perturbed. What do we do when we see a blind man walking toward a cliff? Do we keep quiet because we don't want to disturb or frighten him? If we do, we're guilty of criminal negligence! If we honestly believe in the corrupting influence of sin and the condemnation of God upon it, then we are responsible to warn the world around us of its danger. Our very quality of life should be a beacon of hope to them. That's what it means to be salt.

The Lord Jesus invested a remarkable power in his disciples, the people to whom he was talking here on the mount. John tells us that Jesus said, "Whosoever sins ye remit, they are remitted unto them; and whosoever sins ye retain, they are retained" (20:23). I know there are many interpretations of this power, but I believe Jesus was saying simply this, "If you go out into society and tell people, 'My dear friend, if you refuse to repent, to bow your head and heart before a holy God, if you refuse to acknowledge Jesus Christ as your Savior and Lord, on the authority of the Word of God, you are lost and bound for a Christless eternity,' I will back you up from heaven itself." This is what Jesus' words here in John mean to me. Jesus was asking his disciples to function as salt—to affirm his message of condemnation for sin, but salvation for the repentant.

Salt is a purifier as well. If you've ever had an open cut, you know how salt in that wound made it sting. But it also made it clean. That's another aspect of salt's function—to administer cleansing. There is an interesting reference to the cleansing power of salt in Ezekiel 16:4: "And as for your birth, on the day you were born your navel string was not cut, nor were you washed with water to cleanse you, nor rubbed with salt . . ." (RSV). Salt was used here as part of the cleansing process. What a beautiful, challenging thing it is to be a Christian in the world today. We are to be a means of cleansing. We're not to think of ourselves as better or greater than others because of this call. No, we are servants of the living God as we fulfill this function of being salt.

Salt also has another function. It adds flavor. Job asked the question: "Can that which is unsavory be eaten without salt? or is there any taste in the white of an egg?" (6:6). Did you ever try to eat something that had not been salted to your taste? Flat and unexciting, wasn't it? I'm afraid that's the way many of us Christians come through to the people of the world around us. It's what Jesus was referring to in Mark 9:50: "Salt is good: but if the salt have lost his saltness, wherewith will ye season it? Have salt in yourselves. . . ." He also said, "Salt is good: but if the salt have lost his savor, wherewith shall it be seasoned? It is neither fit for the land, nor yet for the dunghill; but men cast it out . . ." (Luke 14:34,35).

We Christians have no business being boring. Our function is to add flavor and excitement. Jesus was saying in effect, "Does this world have to go on the way it is without salt? Can't we have some salt around here, please, that will add a beautiful touch to the whole thing?" If I as a Christian am boring and dull, if I'm not adding flavor to life around me, I'm not fulfilling my function as salt.

When I was in the Marines, I was the only one in my group who didn't booze it up. Night after night the others would invite me to go out drinking with them, and I would regularly say no to their invitation. Do you know what happened? I became nursemaid and helper, putting them to bed, helping them with their hangovers. At least I added a little touch of difference to the situation. In fact, as the months went by, one by one many of those Marines came to know Christ. I wouldn't settle for the blah and boring life if I could be salt!

The Seriousness of Being Salt

Finally, the seriousness of being salt. This brings us to the "but" of our verse, "Ye are the salt of the earth: *but* if the salt has lost its savor. . . ." Here Jesus is getting around to the importance of fulfilling our function as salt. There is danger, disgrace, and possible disaster here in terms of our Christian testimony. The possibility that the salt may lose its savor was hinted at by Paul in Romans: "Professing themselves to be wise, they became fools" (1:22). Nothing about salt here, is there? In the Greek it's the same word as Jesus used when he pointed out that it is possible for the salt to lose it savor. In Galilee where Jesus lived at this time a cheap grade of salt was used for packing fish. Once it lost its saltness it was useless. If it was spread on the ground, nothing would grow. If it was thrown in the water, it just made the water dirty. This savorless salt was not good for anything. Jesus was saying, "If you're not careful, salt of the earth, you will lose your edge, your distinctiveness, your abrasiveness, your power, your very reason for being." You will become "foolishness" as Paul pointed out in Romans 1 and 1 Corinthians 1. Freely translated, what Jesus was saying is this: "If the salt fools around, it will lose its impact."

Are we as Christians functioning or just fooling around? We can fool around by being more concerned for spiritual complacency than for changing the world for Christ. We can fool around by being more interested in social conformity than spiritual impact. We can also fool around by being more confused morally than any Christian has a right to be. We don't help anyone out of confusion if we are confused ourselves.

I've heard the term "good for nothing" applied to a variety of people. But Jesus applies it to saltless Christians! It's possible for a Christian to fool around so much that he's good for nothing but to be trodden underfoot. His testimony is worthless. Fellow Christian, I want to be salty as a Christian, don't you?

6

The Christian

As the Light of the World

In chapter 5 Jesus referred to Christians as the "salt of the earth." Now he uses another graphic illustration to portray the healthy Christian life. In this book we are concerned with distinctive Christianity, supernormal living. That's what Jesus is calling for in Matthew 5:14–16: "Ye are the light of the world. A city that is set on a hill cannot be hid. Neither do men light a candle, and put it under a bushel, but on a candlestick; and it giveth light unto all that are in the house. Let your light so shine before men, that they may see your good works, and glorify your Father which is in heaven."

Knowing what to believe is one thing. Knowing how to behave is an entirely different matter. But the two are closely related. We need a knowledge of Christian doctrine to understand not only what we believe but also why we believe it. But then we need to know what to do about what we believe. So far we have discovered that Christian behavior is to be quite distinctive. It is something intended to be unique on the face of God's earth. If Christianity is not unique and distinctive, and if Christian behavior, morality, ethics, and living are not abrasive, then they are certainly not what God intended them to be.

We Christians are not only to be "the salt of the earth," we are also to be "the light of the world." In this chapter we will be looking at the various aspects of this subject. First of all, we will examine what Jesus meant by his use of the term "light" to find an *explanation* for it. Then we will deal with the *expectation*—what did Jesus expect to happen in our lives because we are "light"? Finally, we will look at his *exhortation* recorded in verse 16: "Let your light so shine. . . . "

As we pointed out in chapter 5 Jesus is not looking for volunteers or raised hands. He isn't. If he had been, he would have opened his call by saying, "Who would like to be the light of the world?" And he did not say, "What the world needs is lights." He was not offering options; he was making plain statements: "You *are* light" and "You *are* salt." The option is not whether you want to be or not. The only option is: will you function or not? If salt functions, it will not lose its savor. Light cannot function as a light and be hidden under a bucket. The Lord would say to us today as he did to those other disciples, "Look, I'm going to produce in you a distinctive behavior, a totally new way of living that will be as abrasive, effective, and unique as salt on the earth. And I'm going to so work in your life that you're going to be as noticeable as a light shining in a dark place." He made it clear that the possibility of salt losing its saltness and light being hidden exists. But you and I are the salt and the light, and if salt doesn't function and light doesn't shine, then we are failing to be what Jesus called us to be. And we are failing to reach our desperately needy world. I am convinced that unless the church of Jesus Christ really begins to fulfill its function as light and salt, we cannot expect the gospel of Jesus Christ to make an impact on the world.

The Explanation

What did Jesus mean when he said, "You are the light of the world"? First of all, I think he was talking about his disciples having a *continuation* ministry. If we look at what he said in John 8 and 9, this truth begins to emerge: "As long as I am in the world, I am the light of the world" (9:5); "I am the light of the world: he that followeth me shall not walk in darkness, but shall have the light of life" (8:12). Now in Matthew 5:14 he is saying, "Ye are the light of the world." Put those three passages together and what do you have? We are *now* what Christ was *then*. While he was here *he* was the light. Now that he is gone *we* are the light.

We Christians are here in the world to be, through our body universal, local, and individual, nothing more or less than the outshining of the glory of Jesus Christ to a world that lives in darkness. Do you know what our world should be saying simply because it is seeing the lives of Christians? It ought to be saying, "We who live in darkness have seen a great light!" You and I are the lights of the world. If we only begin to understand our lives as a *continuation* of his ministry begun 1900 years ago, how can we condone complacent behavior and excuse our lack of involvement? We are a continuation of his ministry.

Being the "light of the world" gives us a *clarification* ministry as well. When he made the statement, "I am the light of the world," he went on to say, "He that followeth me shall not walk in darkness, but shall have the light of life." When there is a continuation ministry in Christians of that which Christ initiated, we will have followers as he did. People today must find in us such reality, such revelation and truth, such exhilarating excitement, that they will have their darkness banished and begin to understand what it really means to live. Does that idea frighten you? Does it sound heretical? I believe we have a good precedent for thinking this way in the life of the apostle Paul. He was actually able to say, "Be ye followers of me even as I also am of Christ" (1 Cor. 11:1). What was he saying? I follow Jesus Christ, and he is the light of the world. Through his ministry, his life in me, I am becoming something of what he is. Therefore, if you can't see him, look at me. You'll begin to find in and through me something of the glorious person of Jesus Christ. And you can begin to come to grips with him through the ministry I'm having among you.

I find that concept almost terrifying, but that's what Jesus is saying. It's terrifying because it suddenly means that as a Christian, I'm inevitably a marked person. Because of my profession as a Christian, others are going to follow me. And if my profession and my performance do not equate, if my action is not adequate, I will lead them in the wrong way.

You and I are the light of the world. As Christians we are

to be "little Christs." Do some look at us and say, "If that's Christianity, you can keep it"? In many instances people have been turned against the church because of the behavior of the people in the church. They were impressed with Jesus Christ through some unusual experience, but were later singularly unimpressed with those who profess to be his followers. Why? For this very simple reason: We have failed to recognize that we are what he is. We continue what he began. There should be no conflict between our lives and his, no break in his ministry. We should so grasp his principles and so enjoy his life, that his life will flow through us and out to others, performing this clarifying ministry to which I have referred.

This light-giving ministry is the reason we are here. I wonder how the church of Jesus Christ degenerated into a group of people just sitting around congratulating themselves that they are on the way to heaven. What a tragedy!

We also have a ministry of *coordination.* The word here translated as "world" is different from the word "earth" as translated in verse 13, "Ye are the salt of the earth. . . . " You will recall that the word used in verse 13 is the same word from which we get our word "geography." In this earlier verse Jesus was saying, "You've all been placed in the middle of your own little piece of geography. Be salt in that place." Here in verse 14, the word is *Kosmos,* meaning order. The Greek idea of beauty was order. This is the same word from which we get the word "cosmetic." The essence of beauty in the Greek mind was order, balance. God created a system that functions beautifully. He created order and beauty, and man spoiled it. I'm not referring just to what Adam did in the garden; I'm thinking, too, of the ecological mess our world is in today. Because of man's greed which has destroyed the once perfect balance of nature, we're on the brink of ecological disaster. Even the vast regions of space that surround our planet are polluted by man's idiocy. God made the cosmos, and man made chaos.

What is God saying to us? He says, "What I want is order and beauty. And I'm going to bring it by shining through the chaos as the light of the world. You are that light." If I'm going to be that person whose life demonstrates the harmony of God's creation, then coordination must characterize my life, not chaos. That divine quality is going to spill over into my home, my neighborhood, my world. I'm the light of cosmos, the light of order, *the* light.

Does that concept frighten you with its sheer weight of responsibility? I'm frightened by it—but I must recognize my accountability to be a clarifier and a coordinator. Add to these roles my responsibility to continue the ministry Christ began.

Let me paint a picture. Our world is in darkness. Its ships are breaking up on the heavy seas. The storm is rapidly engulfing the vessel. People are going down, and they don't even know where they are. They're lost and confused. Overlooking them is that city set on a hill—the church of Jesus Christ. Even more personally, it's the individual Christian. He is to be steadfast, immovable, inflexible, shining brightly, a light in a dark place. That's what Jesus is calling for here.

Not long ago I was talking to a young lady who expressed her own dissatisfaction with her living arrangements. She told me she wanted to move. I asked her why. "Well," she said, "I'm the only Christian there."

"I still don't understand why you want to move," I replied.

"Because I'm the only Christian there."

"I still don't understand," I persisted.

"It's such a dark place," she explained further.

"It would seem to me that the darker the place the brighter the light that's needed," I answered.

That's what it means to consolidate, to be a reference point, to be a light in the world. The more confusion there is, the greater the need for a solid foundation, one who knows the truth and stands upright for it.

C. T. Studd had an interesting limerick: "Some people like to live within the sound of church or chapel bell. I'd rather run a rescue shop within a yard of hell." They say that Nero fiddled while Rome burned. I wonder how many Christians are fooling around today while people around them are going to hell. You and I are a city set on a hill, the light of the world. We're to be a beacon light to rescue hell-bound sinners around us.

The Expectation

Jesus said, "Neither do men light a candle, and put it under a bushel, but on a candlestick; and it giveth light unto all that are in the house" (v. 15). A simple expectation is expressed here: that bushels will be overturned and candlesticks discovered. There are two definite "bushels," two definite obstacles to our shining as lights: the bushel of indifference and the bushel of inconsistency.

I'm coming down pretty hard here, but one thing that really irritates me is to see an indifferent Christian—because he's the greatest living contradiction you can find. Indifference and Christian just do not belong together. Yet who among us can say truthfully that we don't show indifference every day of our lives? In so doing, we're putting our lights under a bushel; we're a contradiction in terms. And inconsistency is perhaps the most common means of hiding our testimony.

What's the difference between putting our light under a bushel and placing it on a candlestick? A candlestick Christian accepts every opportunity to shine, whereas a bushel Christian hides his light every time he's faced with an opportunity to shine. A candlestick gives the light a very strategic position. As Christians we're not just to blink and twinkle. No, we're to look for the best and most strategic place to function as lights. That's the expectation Jesus has for us. "Get out from under your bushel, and climb up on your candlestick!" he says in no uncertain terms. If I'm to obey his command, I will look for the most strategic place, then I will seek to discover how to shed the most light possible from that place. The expectation is that I will avoid the hidden obstacles, accept the opportunities that come my way, and acknowledge my obligations. That's the way I can let my light shine.

The Exhortation

Now having explained his statement and outlined his expectations, Jesus says, "Let your light so shine before men, that they may see your good works, and glorify your father which is in heaven" (v. 16). To put it in today's terminology, Jesus is saying, "Okay, fellows, get out there and shine!"

First of all, what is to be the method of shining? Jesus spells it out quite clearly and unequivocally—works! That'll shake some of us evangelicals. No, we're not saved by good works, but that doesn't mean we can forget about them. We're saved *unto* good works. James explained the rationale behind that arrangement: "Even so faith, if it hath not works, is dead, being alone. Yea, a man may say, Thou hast faith, and I have works: show me thy faith without thy works, and I will show thee my faith by my works" (2:17,18). To paraphrase James, "If my faith doesn't work, it is highly suspect. It can shout; it can preach; it can thump the pulpit. But if it doesn't work, it's dead." What kind of works? *Good* works. Good works are works that are visible. That doesn't mean just being a nice guy, a good neighbor, a law-abiding citizen. It means much more—standing out from the world around you like a light on a candlestick, a city set on a hill.

Next, let's look at the means of shining. First, kindle the flame! If you have a flicker for a flame, tell the Lord, "I must admit I've been a pretty pathetic light, Lord. All I've produced so far is smoke. Instead of giving people light, I'm afraid I've just offended their nostrils. Set me alight!"

Then "trim the wick"—carefully and regularly work on your life style to remove the grimy deposit of less than satisfactory living.

Thirdly, "replenish the oil"—make sure that you are drawing deeply from the God-given resources made available to you in the Holy Spirit.

Finally, what is our motivation? Does a candle shine merely to be seen? Do candles shine to illuminate other candles? Candles shine to banish darkness. Did you ever see a Christian whose overriding ambition was simply to be seen? Such a person has a real problem. There's too much darkness out there to be concerned about self-glorification. Our works are to glorify our Father in heaven. That's why we are to be lights in the world!

7

The Christian
and the Moral Law

The biblical teaching that God provided an absolute moral standard has been neglected in our modern and enlightened day. And the results are clearly seen in the moral chaos all around us. A clear restatement of God's moral law is imperative at this particular time. Many people are deeply concerned about the great upsurge of immorality in our day. Frankly, I'm not as concerned about immorality as I am about the rise of amorality. Immorality is the breaking of a moral standard, but amorality simply says that there is no such thing as a moral standard. It seems to me that this attitude is our real danger in the world today.

We live in a society that says there is no such thing as an absolute moral standard. A classic example of that kind of thinking is the recent development of conflicting pornography legislation. The highest court in the land has pulled a real cop-out in this matter. The Supreme Court now tells us that it is up to the local area to determine what is pornographic, throwing the whole situation into utter and unmanageable confusion. The point I'm making is simply this: we live in a society that says in effect, "It's really up to everyone to decide his own moral standards. And if you don't have any, that's all right, too. Just don't bother anyone else, because we're all free to make up our own minds!"

This is in total opposition to the clear teachings of the Scriptures. The Bible tells us that God is the author of morality, that he is a moral being, and that he has legislated certain moral standards without which no society can exist in right relationship with him or each other. An absence of a solid moral foundation is an invitation to moral chaos.

The Importance of the Moral Law

Early in his Sermon on the Mount the Lord Jesus came out in strong defense of the moral law of God. In Matthew 5:17 he said, "Think not that I am come to destroy the law, or the prophets: I am not come to destroy, but to fulfil. . . . " The law to which he was referring here was the law given on Mt. Sinai by revelation to Moses, what we commonly call the Ten Commandments recorded in Exodus 20.

First of all, the importance of the moral law lies in the fact that it was *enacted by God.* "And God spake all these words, saying, I am the Lord thy God, which have brought thee out of the land of Egypt, out of the house of bondage" (Exod. 20:1,2). Following this introduction God goes on to give the ten basic statements that are the core of his moral law. This is still God's principle of morality and is just as relevant for us today as it was for the world into which it came thousands of years ago. One of the crying needs of our world is simply to be reminded of this fact: God is a moral being who has given us an uncompromising moral standard that relates and applies to life today.

There are two important truths for us to see in this moral law. First, it is a revelation of the being of God. He says, "I am the Lord thy God. . . . " Some people seem to think they can break the law simply because they do not like the lawmakers! Such people are putting the lawmaker into a class with themselves, making him no better than themselves. God nips that kind of thinking in the bud when he identifies himself right here at the outset. No one can adopt this kind of an attitude toward God, for the very preamble of his law reveals that he is the One from whom all things come.

Secondly, God makes it clear that he is not about to share his glory with anyone. The first commandment states unequivocally, "Thou shalt have no other gods before me" (Exod. 20:3). This is the Supreme Being speaking, and he is no remote, obscure deity; he is the One who led Israel out of Egypt. His law is a legitimate requirement of those whom he has created and sustained.

After firmly establishing his identity as God, he goes on to deal with every aspect of Godward and manward relationships. No area of our lives is left unclarified. After clarifying man's responsibilities Godward, he deals with interpersonal relationships. He instituted the family and lays down some rules for keeping the family structure inviolate. He created man and insists that man recognize the sanctity of human life. All things were made by him and he insists on man's right to own and protect property. These are God's requirements for human behavior, and they call for moral decisions on our part.

Society in general is in danger of totally rejecting God's clear standards set forth in the Ten Commandments. The church of Jesus Christ and individual Christians need to stand up and be counted on this matter: God's law is as relevant today as when it was delivered to Moses thousands of years ago. The divine standards of moral behavior are not out of date!

How can I consider myself a normal Christian and cheat on my income tax? Or betray the sanctity of the marriage bond? Or disregard the principle of the Lord's Day? Or provide a poor example of Christianity to my children and neighbors? The tragedy is that not only has society in general laid the Lord's law in ruins, but so-called Christians are also guilty of rejecting the divine rulebook. That is why society is rapidly disintegrating around us. Every man has become a law unto himself.

The moral law of God is important not only because it was enacted by God himself, but also because it was *enforced by the prophets*. In Matthew 5:17 Jesus links the two: "Think not that I am come to destroy the law, or the prophets. . . . " Not only was the law enacted by God, but down through Israel's history it had been enforced by the prophets. One after another, they had reiterated God's message, reinforcing it by their teachings and example.

Perhaps what we need today is a visitation from an old-time

prophet! Moses, for instance. In Deuteronomy 30:16 Moses said, "In that I command thee this day to love the Lord thy God, to walk in his ways, and to keep his commandments and his statutes, and his judgments...." In Verse 19 he adds, "...that I have set before you life and death, blessing and cursing: therefore choose life, that both thou and thy seed may live." Two words stand out in these verses: *command* and *choose*. They are the essence of the enforcing message of the prophets. God has enunciated moral standards which are his commands, his requirements for living. Men must choose whether to obey him or disobey. Jesus did not depart from this standard set forth by God and reinforced by Moses. He supported it!

Look at Isaiah. At the beginning of his prophecy he said, "Come now, and let us reason together, saith the Lord; though your sins be as scarlet, they shall be as white as snow; though they be red like crimson, they shall be as wool. If ye be willing and obedient, ye shall eat the good of the land: But if ye refuse and rebel, ye shall be devoured with the sword: for the mouth of the Lord hath spoken it" (1:18,19). Either you are willing and obedient, or you refuse and rebel. Here it is not a communication of command and choice; it is a message of obey or disobey. Have you ever heard someone excuse his way of flaunting the law of God by saying, "I'm not living under law— I'm under grace"? What a travesty on the meaning of grace. Freedom from the law does not mean license to do as I please. It means I now obey God out of love for him, rather than out of fear of his wrath.

Let's look at one other prophet—Malachi. "Even from the days of your fathers ye are gone away from mine ordinances, and have not kept them. Return unto me, and I will return unto you, saith the Lord of hosts. But ye said, Wherein shall we return? Will a man rob God? Yet ye have robbed me.... Bring ye all the tithes into the storehouse..." (3:7–10). God is hitting the people where it hurts. They have broken the first commandment, "Thou shalt have no other gods before me." Also, they have operated contrary to his commandment, "Thou shalt not steal." God's moral law is simple, and it is broken in every pew of every church in the land. God says we should not covet, but we covet so much that we cannot support the work of God.

We could say the same about the other seven commandments. We break them all in some way. And the prophets are
simply reemphasizing what God said when he made his covenant with man. Through Malachi God is saying, "Either return unto me, or you are rejecting my principles." Do we dare
answer as did the people of Malachi's day: "It is vain to serve
God: and what profit is it that we have kept his ordinance, and
that we have walked mournfully before the Lord of hosts"
(3:14)? When we refuse to obey him, that's what we're doing.

As we look at Jesus in the Bible, we see him in many roles.
But I'm afraid that we usually fail to see him as the endorser
of God's law. He endorsed it by his life in that he totally affirmed its validity: "And he that sent me is with me: the
Father hath not left me alone; for I do always those things
that please him" (John 8:29). Every day we Christians are
faced with opportunities to please the Father. Every time we
say no to the temptation to lie, steal, or commit adultery, we
are pleasing him. Why do we stand true? Because we love
God more than the sin we are tempted to commit. If you want
to please the Father as Jesus did, live your life as Jesus did, a
total endorsement of the moral law. Notice what he said later
in his Sermon: "Therefore all things whatsoever ye would that
men should do to you, do ye even so to them: for this is *the
law and the prophets*" (Matt. 7:12 *italics mine*). We glibly
sum up this verse as the "golden rule"—but Jesus says the
golden rule is nothing more or less than the total fulfillment of
the law and the prophets.

Jesus Christ not only totally endorsed the validity and ve-
racity of the moral law by fulfilling it in his life and amplify-
ing it in his teaching, he also acknowledged it by his death. In
Galatians 3:13 Paul says, "Christ hath redeemed us from the
curse of the law, being made a curse for us: for it is written,
Cursed is every one that hangeth on a tree." If you want to
know what Christ thought of the law, look at him on the cross.
Why did he endure the shame and pain of the cross? Because
of the rank immorality and amorality of fallen humanity who
had totally rejected God's law. Jesus Christ was made to be
sin for us, because of his estimate of that law.

One final point: I see the *endorsement of Christ* on the
moral law because it is answered by his Spirit: "That the right-

eousness of the law might be fulfilled in us, who walk not
after the flesh, but after the Spirit" (Rom. 8:4). Do you know
that the Bible actually teaches that Jesus endorsed this law so
utterly and completely that he affirmed it by his life, amplified it by his teaching, acknowledged it by his death, and answers every demand of the moral law in the life of every person who lives in the fullness of the Holy Spirit?

We speak in hushed tones of living the Spirit-filled life. Do
you know what it is? The Spirit-filled life is simply living a
life before God and among men according to the moral law of
a moral God. We may call it the fruit of the Spirit: love, joy,
peace, longsuffering, gentleness, goodness, faith, meekness,
and temperance, but it means the same thing. God is a unity,
and he's saying one thing loud and clear: "I'm a moral being;
this is my moral law. You've broken it, but Christ died that
you might be forgiven. And he has come to live within you by
his Holy Spirit that you might operate according to my stated
plan: the total and unequivocal fulfillment of the law."
There is no way for us to call ourselves normal Christians,
Spirit-filled Christians, if we are not fulfilling the moral law.
That's how important it is. Now let's look at

The Permanence of the Moral Law

Jesus spelled it out for us: "For verily I say unto you, Till
heaven and earth pass, one jot or one tittle shall in no wise
pass from the law, till all be fulfilled" (Matt. 5:18). Jesus was
saying that the law is totally and utterly permanent. He pref-
aced it with the authoritative, "Verily." Other translations
say, "Truly." This was an authoritative statement, backed up
by all that Jesus is.

Not only that, but it was also an absolute standard. The
theory of relativism is popular in considering behavior today.
Fletcher calls it "situation ethics." He makes moral questions
"relative." What is wrong today may be right tomorrow, if
the circumstances change. This reminds me of our dilemma
with the pornography legislation with which we opened this
chapter. Such fuzzy thinking leads us into a chaos of confusion. Was Joseph wrong for not giving in to the wiles of the
woman who tempted him (Gen. 39:7 ff.)? After all, she was

his master's wife, and his job may have depended upon it! No, Joseph did not fall into the trap. He followed an absolute standard: God's law. Not one jot or tittle would pass in his life style. He chose to obey God rather than follow the route of expediency.

The Relevance of the Moral Law

"Whosoever therefore shall break one of these least commandments, and shall teach men so, he shall be called the least in the kingdom of heaven: but whosoever shall do and teach them, the same shall be called great in the kingdom of heaven" (Matt. 5:19). The moral law of God is a principle of behavior for those who are in the kingdom. Jesus says, "If you as a Christian in the kingdom are going to be disobedient in the least area of the moral law, and teach people either by your words or actions that they can deny the moral law with impunity, you will be the least in the kingdom." We have an equation here: Disobedience + denial = disgrace. The moral law is relevant to the Christian.

Jesus then goes on to show the results of obedience: " . . . whosoever shall do and teach them, the same shall be called great in the kingdom of heaven." Here is another equation: Doing plus disseminating equals distinction. We have a choice. Will we be great in the kingdom—or a disgrace? We choose by our attitude toward the moral law of God.

Not only is God's moral law relevant as a principle of Christian behavior, it is also relevant as a prelude to Christian conversion. Jesus makes that clear in Matthew 5:20: "For I say unto you, That except your righteousness shall exceed the righteousness of the scribes and Pharisees, ye shall in no case enter into the kingdom of heaven." Now he is speaking not to those in the kingdom, but to those still outside. The moral law helps us understand the fallacy of our own self-righteousness. The problem with the scribes and Pharisees, to whom these words were addressed, was this: they were so meticulous in their observance of the letter of the law, that they missed the whole spirit of the law. Their attitude meant that they completely lacked the true spirit of worship for which God longs.

This is what makes the moral law so helpful as a prelude to

Christian conversion. It helps me recognize and reject my own self-righteousness. It reveals my unrighteousness. If I break one tiny aspect of God's law, I'm guilty of breaking it all. But the beautiful thing about it is this: When I admit my unrighteousness, and my self-righteousness, when I come before God broken in repentance, asking for forgiveness, no matter what my sin is, I'm forgiven. God's law is just, but God is a merciful, loving Judge.

8

The Christian

and Anger

So far in the Sermon on the Mount Jesus has been dealing in generalities, but beginning in verse 24 he becomes very specific, as he applies the moral law, "Thou shalt not kill." The implications of this commandment unfold like a flower before our eyes, as he begins to show us the broad intent of this prohibition against murder. In this chapter we will be dealing with three areas of truth. First:

Some Basic Assumptions Jesus Makes

At this point in his Sermon Jesus assumes that his hearers know the moral law. Ignorance of the law cannot be used by them as an excuse any longer. He states it this way: "Ye have heard that it was said by them of old time, Thou shalt not kill; and whosoever shall kill shall be in danger of the judgment" (Matt 5:21). I think there are two reasons why Jesus could make this assumption.

First of all, Jewish parents were duty-bound to teach their children the law of God. "And these words, which I command thee this day, shall be in thine heart: And thou shalt teach them diligently unto thy children, and shalt talk of them when thou sittest in thine house, and when thou walkest by the way, and when thou liest down, and when thou risest up. And thou

shalt bind them for a sign upon thine hand, and they shall be
as frontlets between thine eyes. And thou shalt write them
upon the posts of thy house, and on thy gates" (Deut. 6:6–9).
Parents have a moral and spiritual obligation to teach their
children God's standard of conduct. Pastors, Sunday school
teachers, and youth counselors cannot do it all.

One of the great problems in our country today is simply
this: parents are not fulfilling their God-given roles. God's
blueprint for the home is a program of teaching by the parents, particularly the fathers, which is to be reinforced by the
church, the school, and other areas of influence. This does not
mean a desultory prayer occasionally, or a perfunctory "Don't
forget your Bible reading" as the kids drag themselves from
the TV and head for bed. Rather, it means doing the sort of
thing that happened as recorded in Nehemiah 8:8, "So they
read in the book in the law of God distinctly, and gave the
sense, and caused them to understand the reading." Notice
that not only was the reading distinct, but the teachers also
gave the sense and caused the people to understand what was
read.

This is why Jesus assumed that the people knew the moral
law, for they should have heard it in their homes and in their
churches. Both parents and preachers were to fulfill their obligations.

The second assumption that Jesus makes is that the people
not only have a knowledge of the law of God, but they also
have a respect for it. They believe it, and they believe it in a
realistic way. There are three basic reasons why people respect the law of God:

First, they respect it because of its *source*—God himself. If
we believe in a Supreme Being (and most people do in one
way or another), and we believe that he has given us principles of behavior and operation, for that reason alone we must
have unbelievable respect for his law. How can we treat something of divine origin without respect? Then there is the *scope*
of his law. The Ten Commandments touch people in every
area of their beings, in every conceivable aspect of their existence. God has spoken to the issues and dealt with the problems that confront us. Nothing is left unsaid.

Finally, we should respect the law because of its *severity.*

Not only does God clearly outline his requirements for Christian behavior, he also spells out in no uncertain terms what will happen to the people if they do not play the game according to his rules. God firmly believes in deterrents—that which will frighten a person into acting in a certain way because he realizes what will happen to him if he doesn't. There is abroad in our world today what is known as a "nuclear deterrent." The United States has a nuclear capability, and so does Russia. The idea seems to be that as long as our abilities parallel each other, both sides will avoid war because of its terrible consequences in human life and devastation. That is a nuclear deterrent. God's moral law operates in somewhat the same fashion. God says, "I am the Lord your God. These are my principles. Do them and you will live. Don't and you will perish." That breeds respect for the law of God, and Jesus assumed that.

Some Bold Assertions Jesus Makes

Jesus makes several assertions that are shattering in their implications. He claims here that his words and the law of God demand equal attention. There are people who make much of the "revealed will of God" and who are deeply impressed by "the law of Moses"—they think these are the bases upon which a civilized society must be built. But they have no time for the sayings of Jesus Christ. Here in Matthew 5:22 Jesus claims equal status: "But I say unto you. . . ." There is no question but that the people got the message, for at the end of the Sermon (Matt. 7:29) we are told: "For he taught them as one having authority, and not as the scribes." The authority with which Jesus Christ spoke made the people sit up and take notice.

What am I trying to say? There are plenty of people who believe implicitly in "Thou shalt not kill," but they do not believe "That whosoever is angry with his brother without a cause shall be in danger of the judgment" (Matt. 5:22). They don't believe that anger toward a brother is murder—but Jesus says it is! And that's not all. His second bold assertion is that anger and killing merit equal punishment: "Ye have heard that it was said by them of old time, Thou shalt not kill;

and whosoever shall kill shall be in danger of the judgment: *But I say unto you,* That whosoever is angry with his brother . . . shall be in danger of the judgment: and whosoever shall say to his brother, Raca, shall be in danger of the council: but whosoever shall say, Thou fool, shall be in danger of hell fire" (Matt. 5:21,22). The word judgment refers to certain crimes for which men could be brought up before the local courts. The next highest court was the council, the Sanhedrin, which met in Jerusalem. Anger is a sin which merits the attention of that tribunal. But even more striking is Jesus' crowning claim: anger is a sin worthy of the final judgment.

Wait a minute! Did Jesus really say that? Did he say, "If you get mad, you're going to hell"? No, he was speaking figuratively here. He is saying that local judgment, that even higher judgment, and the most severe judgment of all, hell fire, are deserved by the angry man. In this, he was bucking the popular sentiment which excuses anger, glossing it over, making it less serious than it really is. But anger leads to murder, so Jesus was saying, "I take anger so seriously that I believe it is to be weighed in the same balance as murder."

Not only does he point out that anger and killing merit equal punishment, but he proceeds to give us some reasons for this judgment. First of all, anger is murder's root. Look at the murder statistics in our own country and in Northern Ireland. More people were murdered in the city of Detroit last year than were killed in the whole of Northern Ireland. But here's a striking fact. Most of the murders committed in the United States were committed by one family member against another. Someone lost his temper, went for a gun, and murder was the result. That is one reason Jesus comes down so heavily on the subject of anger. It leads to murder. The case of Cain and Abel is a classic example of how the heart filled with anger can erupt into violence against one's brother.

Anger can involve something other than the body, however. It can destroy an individual's personhood. The word, "Raca," in verse 22 means, "You are utterly worthless. I despise you." Later in the verse, Jesus uses the expression, "Thou fool," which in our parlance today would be like saying,"You're stupid." This attitude is destructive of the personhood of the individual at the receiving end of the judgment. Downgrading your fellow man who is made in the image of God is a form of murder, and Jesus condemns this attitude among others in his blanket statement, "Whosoever therefore shall break one of these least commandments, and shall teach men so, he shall be called the least in the kingdom of heaven . . ." (Matt. 5:19). This applies to Christians, who have known the forgiveness of God, just as appropriately as to the non-Christian. Who is the least in the kingdom? The person who is a Christian, but in his personal relationships does not control his temper, who lashes out with his tongue, intent on reducing another person to nothingness. Anger kills personhood.

Anger also destroys brotherhood. According to Romans 13, the whole essence of the law of God is love. There is no way that anger can portray love. Neither adultery or lying reveal love in any way. Blasphemy certainly reveals anything but love. And one thing Jesus is impressing upon his hearers is this: "If there is anything that will wreck the brotherhood of believers and the personhood of all people, it is anger—which leads to insult, which leads to the destruction of human beings. Watch out for it!"

Here's a paradox for you, however. In some instances, killing may not be sin. Undeniably, the Old Testament teaches or endorses capital punishment. "He that smiteth a man, so that he die, shall be surely put to death. . . . And he that smiteth his father, or his mother, shall be surely put to death. . . . Eye for eye, tooth for tooth, hand for hand, foot for foot, Burning for burning, wound for wound, stripe for stripe" (Exod. 21:12, 15,24,25).

That isn't all. Even anger may not be sin. "Be ye angry, and sin not . . ." (Eph. 4:26). This is another of the bold exceptions Jesus makes. If your anger is self-centered, it is sin. On the other hand, if you don't get angry sometimes for the sake of other people, that can be sin as well. Jesus became angry when other people's rights were violated, or when the house of God was desecrated (John 2:16). Nehemiah became angry at the exploitation of the common people by their leaders (5: 1–8). Social injustice upset him to the point where he said, "I was very angry when I heard their cry and these words." In both instances I've quoted, however, this anger was not a light thing. It developed because of injustice done not to the speaker, not to the one who was angry, but to others.

Some Big Actions Jesus Expects of Us

First of all, Jesus expects us to *recognize* sin for what it is. We must take note of the causes of anger: "For from within, out of the heart of men, proceed evil thoughts, adulteries, fornications, murders . . ." (Mark 7:21). What causes anger? A sinful heart. Pride also causes anger: "And he was angry, and would not go in . . ." (Luke 15:28). The elder son was jealous of the celebration put on by his father when the prodigal brother returned from his rebellious wandering. His pride was hurt and he refused to participate in the welcome-home party. He was jealous of the recognition given his brother—and the lack of recognition given him. We fail to handle our anger if we fail to recognize it for what it is.

We also need to recognize its characteristics. Did you ever, as a husband, want to get even with your wife? Or did you, as a wife, ever want to get back at your husband? That's the spirit Paul was exposing in Ephesians 4:30–32: "And grieve not the Holy Spirit of God, whereby ye are sealed unto the day of redemption. Let all bitterness, and wrath, and anger, and clamor, and evil speaking, be put away from you, with all malice: and be ye kind one to another, tender-hearted, forgiving one another, even as God for Christ's sake hath forgiven you." All these actions are characteristic of one sin: anger. All the reactions Paul calls for in verse 32 are the result of one character of fruit in the life: love. Bitterness, wrath, anger, clamor, evil speaking, malice—all these are healed and counteracted by love. All of them grieve the Holy Spirit, but love fulfills his will in our lives.

Then we need to *reject* anger's hold upon our lives. Paul says, "But now ye also put off all these; anger, wrath, malice, blasphemy, filthy communication out of your mouth. Lie not one to another, seeing that ye have put off the old man with his deeds" (Col. 3:8,9). In other words, Paul is saying, these old deeds of the "old man" have nothing to do with the new nature. Reject them. How? Understand what is wrong and say no to it. Understand what is right and say yes to it. If you become angry, it isn't because you cannot help it. It's because you *want* to get angry. If you get angry and *stay* angry, it isn't because of the terrible provocation you have suffered, it's because you are being disobedient.

The third big action is *reconciliation.* "Be ye angry, and sin not. Let not the sun go down upon your wrath." How do you deal with anger? Daily. The problem has to be resolved before sunset. Recognize it.

Men, if you come to church angry at your wife, leave immediately. Get right with her outside the church. Then come in and bring your gift. That's my practical paraphrase of Matthew 5:23 and Ephesians 4:26. If we were to examine the myriad of marital problems rampant in the church today, we would discover that anger lies at the root, anger shown in bitterness, resentment, and hatred. If these roots had been dealt with on a biblical basis, saying yes to the Spirit of God and no to sin, divorce would not have reached epidemic proportions in the church as it has. I firmly believe this. If reconciliation had been sought before the going down of the sun every day, the breakdown of "Christian" marriages would not have happened. We don't solve the problem by looking at the provocation and excusing the anger; we solve it by looking deep within ourselves, at our own sinful hearts, and dealing with what we see there. Anger is one of the most common sins overcoming the Christian. We must give our angers to the Lord and let his Spirit fill our lives.

9

The Christian
and Sex

Ye have heard that it was said by them of old time, Thou shalt
not commit adultery: But I say unto you, That whosoever
looketh on a woman to lust after her hath committed adultery
with her already in his heart. And if thy right eye offend thee,
pluck it out, and cast it from thee: for it is profitable for thee
that one of thy members should perish, and not that thy whole
body should be cast into hell. And if thy right hand offend thee,
cut it off, and cast it from thee: for it is profitable for thee that
one of thy members should perish, and not that thy whole body
should be cast into hell (Matt. 5:27–30).

These are unquestionably some of the most hard-hitting
words our Lord spoke in the whole of his very provocative Sermon on the Mount. This passage contains some of his clearest
teachings on the subject of sex. As we look into this whole
area I want to deal with it biblically, honestly, and openly.

It is vitally important that the Christian understand sex as
a dynamic, driving force of human life. In our modern day
this God-given gift is abused rather than used as God planned
it. Terrible sin, degradation, and unbelievable problems riddle
our world because of this misuse. The power of anger, which
we discussed in chapter 8, and the power of sex are two of the
most dynamic forces operative in human experience. Chris-

tians especially must not only know how to cope with anger, they must also know how to handle sex. Their positive example in dealing with these two forces is vitally important if our Christian witness is to be effective in the world. A godly example is desperately needed. In this chapter we will be looking at some biblical teachings on sex, some alternative theories about sex, and Jesus' teachings in particular on the subject.

Biblical Teachings on Sex

Sex is a fact of life—and I'm not referring to those often embarrassed exchanges between father and son and mother and daughter at the onset of puberty and its mysteries. I'm referring to the fact that sexuality *is* a *divine creation*, planned by God for the human race he instituted: "So God created man in his own image, in the image of God created he him; male and female created he them" (Gen.1:27). Notice, the very differences in human sexuality were part of God's divine plan. This is not a subject for embarrassment or "under-the-counter" exploitation. It's an exalted area of life when used in line with God's stated rules.

Not only is sexuality a divine creation, but also sexual activity is a *divine command*: "And God blessed them, and God said unto them, Be fruitful, and multiply, and replenish the earth . . ." (Gen. 1:28). I realize this approach to the subject is not typical of what happens in many church circles today, where sex education is relegated to the schoolyard or the secular schoolroom. Both media are generally condemned by Christians for giving a false perspective and emphasis. But unfortunately the church either treats the subject with benign respect or takes a negative view of this area of life about which God is very positive and clear-cut. The Bible offers us a solid, sane understanding and a healthy appreciation of sex, if we will only search it out and apply it.

Another thing we should notice—sexual activity is a *divine concern*: "And the Lord God said, It is not good that the man should be alone; I will make him an help meet for him" (Gen. 2:18). So important and vital is the union between man and woman that God goes on to say: "Therefore shall a man leave his father and his mother, and shall cleave unto his wife: and they shall be one flesh" (Gen. 2:24). What is God saying? "Adam, you should not be alone. You need someone with whom to share your life. I will give you a woman to complete you." That's what the word, "helpmeet," or "helpmate" means—companion and helper. And the strange term, "one flesh," refers, among other things, to the physical side of the marriage relationship. It really concerns God when two people come together in marriage, but have an unhealthy sexual relationship. It also concerns him when two people have a sexual life outside the marriage bond, for that is also contrary to his will. There is no question about it: according to the Bible sex is a fact of life.

Note this as well: *sex is a facet of love. Facet* is a lovely word used to describe one of the surfaces of a cut gem. For example, a diamond has many such surfaces, enhancing its beauty and luster. Love, too, has many facets, and sex is just one of them. Our problem in society today is that we have tended to make sex and love synonymous, confusing the two, putting the idea of love into the wrong perspective.

In Greek thought, love is represented by three different words: *agape, philia*, and *eros*. The first word is used to describe God's love, a love which is supposed to operate in the Christian's life because he is indwelt by the Holy Spirit. This is the kind of love which sent the Savior to the cross. It is to so permeate the Christian's life that it overflows upon all those with whom he comes in contact, regardless of how they in turn treat him.

The second kind of love, *philia*, is a brotherly love, a social kind of love, another facet of the concept of love. People who have no sense of the living God within them can and do show this kind of love. They have a concern for people. Often we Christians are put to shame by this kind of love as evidenced in the lives of unbelievers.

There is a third kind of love—*eros*. This is the Greek word from which we get our English word, "erotic." It is not found in the Bible, and it refers to sexual love. You might remember these three kinds of love by thinking of them as sacred (or spiritual), social (or secular), and sexual. All three kinds of love are to be operative in the life of the Christian, and all three are to be present in the marriage relationship. The needs of two people, man and woman, in all three of these areas are to be met by the "one flesh" marriage relationship. Any union less than this will be less than biblical love, God's best and total plan for humanity.

When two young people come to me wanting to marry each other, one of the first areas I question is their spiritual condition. This usually surprises them, and often they wonder aloud what this has to do with marriage in general and their wedding in particular. My answer to them is summed up in the preceding paragraph. Marriage between Christians implies spiritual unity, social unity, and sexual unity. Anything less is not in accord with God's divine plan. I'm not talking about people who are not united in spiritual love because one became a Christian after they were married. I'm talking about the disunity that exists when a person who claims to know *agape* (spiritual) love marries someone who is dead in that area of life. The Bible forbids it, and I know it just does not work. It is marriage less than the biblical model.

I know of other couples whose marriages have broken down because the *philia* aspect of love is absent in their lives. The social dimension is also necessary to total marriage. Marriage demands constant adjustment and adaptation, a growing attitude of oneness between maturing people who love each other.

Where does *eros* fit in here? Sexual love is intended to be the very physical demonstration of spiritual love. It is also the underpinning for social love. You cannot divorce any of these aspects of love from the other two. A fullness of love is found in a union of all three. Let me illustrate this truth from the experience of Adam and Eve: "And Adam knew Eve his wife; and she conceived, and bare Cain, and said, I have gotten a man from the Lord" (Gen. 4:1). The word "knew" in this context describes the idea of absolute union. The Living Bible uses the term, "sexual intercourse," to render this word in our modern terminology. It simply means that in every conceivable area of their lives there was a oneness. They were two human beings spiritually, socially, and sexually united, who knew each other at every level of their lives, and this knowledge was consummated in one pinnacle experience that crowned the whole glorious relationship.

Contrast their experience with much of what constitutes sexual behavior today. Sex on the purely human level (without the divine dimension) becomes animal behavior because it does not involve getting to know a whole person. It involves getting and having another person's *body*, but not that person's inner essence.

Lest you assume that I'm calling for all-out sexual activity, let me sound a warning note here. The Bible teaches that sex is a force that can get out of control. These basic drives built into us by our Creator can lead to danger if they get out of control. For example, the hunger drive is needed for survival —but out of control it can mean a glutton's death. The same is true of the sex drive. Out of control in the human race, it could lead to chaos. Unlicensed, uncontrolled sexual activity would destroy the human race. This leads us to the control area spelled out by Jesus in the Sermon on the Mount: "Ye have heard that it was said by them of old time, Thou shalt not commit adultery" (Matt. 5:27). This is God's regulation for handling the potential chaos of uncontrolled sexuality. It is not simply a negative restriction. It is a controlling mechanism for insuring that society will continue to function.

One of our problems in this modern day arises from our rejection of God's demand for the sanctity of sex in the marriage relationship. Adultery and every other kind of sexual sin are running rampant through our world. This leads me to look at three common theories of sexual activity set up as alternatives to the Bible's teachings on the subject:

Alternative Theories about Sex

Three alternative theories are worthy of note here: the Victorian ethic, the Playboy ethic, and the permissive ethic. In grouping Victorianism with the other two points of view here I do not mean to imply that the Victorian ethic belongs on the same level. It appears here as simply an alternative to the biblical view. I do not intend that it be condemned on the same scale of severity. But the Victorian attitude toward sex is as non-biblical as the other two. To the Victorian, sex was something shameful, something nice people did not do. Not only was it shameful and naughty, it implied depravity on the part of the participants in the act. Because this attitude makes sexual activity sinful, it is anti-biblical. The Bible says, "Drink waters out of thine own cistern, and running waters out of thine own well. Let thy fountains be dispersed abroad, and rivers of waters in the streets. Let them be only thine own, and not strangers' with thee. Let thy fountain be blessed: and rejoice with the wife of thy youth. Let her be as the loving hind and pleasant roe; let her breasts satisfy thee at all times; and be thou ravished always with her love" (Prov. 5:15–19). The Song of Solomon is another glowing description of the beauties and ecstasies of marital love. The Victorian ethic rejects these teachings about sex and in so doing is unbiblical, even anti-biblical in its emphasis.

The second alternative is the so-called Playboy ethic, which is just the opposite of the Victorian ethic. To the follower of this philosophy, sex is not shameful, it is fun—and our goal should be to have as much fun as possible. All this emphasis on the "fun" aspects makes me think of children playing in a sandbox. No doubt in your town there are "adult" bookstores —but that is a misnomer. Those who frequent such places are not showing maturity or adult behavior. They are demonstrating that the "sex is fun" philosophy produces not men but infants, not maturity but immaturity, people unable to understand sex in its proper perspective. The Victorian is out in left field, and the Playboy is out in right field. The truth lies in center field, which we will look at later in the chapter.

The Victorian ethic is anti-biblical, and the Playboy ethic is anti-social—for one reason: it results in hedonism, the doctrine that pleasure or happiness is the highest good. Hedonism looks for pleasure to satisfy itself; it is basically selfish and self-seeking. Any person whose thinking is dominated by selfishness will ultimately end up as an anti-social individual, seeking his own pleasure at the expense of the well-being of others. This Playboy philosophy if allowed to rule our world would result in chaos.

The third philosophy is the permissive ethic. The reasoning behind this ethic assumes that sex is merely natural. It is a mistake to restrict what comes naturally. Man is just like an animal in this regard, acting on his natural instincts. To regulate his sex drives is to put unhealthy and unnatural limitations upon him which will restrict him unduly, creating frustration and needless unhappiness. This is the platform of the permissive ethic. Where does this kind of thinking lead us? It produces what I call perverted alliances.

The first of these is the alliance of premarital sex. Sex is meant to be the pinnacle, the consummation of a total relationship: spiritual, social, and sexual. There is no way for two people before marriage to reach this kind of an in-depth knowledge of one another. Such a relationship demands total commitment, a commitment that cannot exist between people unwilling to commit themselves to the marriage bond.

The second area is the alliance of extramarital sex. This is another product of the permissive society. The biblical ideal of marriage calls for two people to "leave" and "cleave," forming a new entity by their sexual unity. Any violation of that unity in terms of "extramarital" involvements is a perversion of God's plan and purpose for marriage.

A third perverted alliance is homosexuality. Our permissive attitude in society has spawned a monster that is even now rearing its ugly head above our country seeking whom it may devour. The Bible is clear in its condemnation of this perverted practice. To cite just one passage: "For this reason [because of their rejection of God] God gave them up to dishonorable passions. Their women exchanged natural relations for unnatural, and the men likewise gave up natural relations with women and were consumed with passion for one another, men committing shameless acts with men and receiving in their own persons the due penalty for their error" (Rom. 1:26,27 RSV). Homosexuality militates against God's ordained family unit, just as do the previous alliances cited. I consider it to be totally anti-Christian. The family unit is the basic unit in the fabric of society, and these perverted forces are designed to weaken if not completely destroy that unit. We need to understand what these alternative approaches to human sexuality are saying. And now let us look at:

The Christian Treatment of Sex

Believe it or not, the Christian is the only person who can find the total delight in the sexual experience that God has planned for his children. Commitment to Jesus Christ and complete enjoyment of sexual joy are not incompatible. The only restriction Jesus places upon this relationship between man and woman is that it take place within the confines of marriage. Paul tells us, ". . . let every man have his own wife, and let every woman have her own husband" (1 Cor. 7:2). Here is a simple statement of fact calling for delight in the sexual relationship within the bonds of marriage.

Notice another aspect of this intimate relationship: it is to be enjoyed on the *level of mutuality*: "Let the husband render unto the wife due benevolence: and likewise also the wife unto the husband. The wife hath not power of her own body, but the husband: and likewise also the husband hath not power of his own body, but the wife. Defraud ye not one the other, except it be with consent for a time . . . " (1 Cor. 7:3–5). If we are looking for a biblical basis for sex life in marriage, this is it. Sexual fulfillment is in God's design for the marriage relationship.

The second thing Jesus is calling for is the exercise of sexual discipline which fulfills the command, "Thou shalt not commit adultery." In Matthew 5:28 he says, "But I say unto you, That whosoever looketh on a woman to lust after her hath committed adultery with her already in his heart." There is such a thing as lust in a look. The experience of sexual delight is biblically valid and necessary, but the exercise of sexual discipline is also biblically necessary. The discipline starts with real discernment. Jesus is saying, "Fornication is not just a physical act. It is a mental attitude." Love longs to give, but lust says, "I love me, and I'm going to get this woman for me." I believe this is particularly but not exclusively a problem for men, and that's why I say it this way.

In addition to discipline in this area, we also need to respect the principle of denial. Jesus is very explicit on this point: "And if thy right eye offend thee, pluck it out, and cast it from thee: for it is profitable for thee that one of thy members should perish, and not that thy whole body should be cast into hell" (Matt. 5:29). What is Jesus saying here? That we should follow his command literally? No, I don't believe so, for where would we stop with this self-mutilation? After the right eye, would the left eye have to go? What about the man who can be turned on by the smell of perfume? Does he cut off his nose? Or the seductive sound of a woman's voice? Does he cut off his ear? Sexual arousal can come from any one of our senses, and Jesus is calling for us to control our senses and *deny* ourselves in all these areas—not to *destroy* our senses. He's not saying we must get rid of every one of our senses, but he *is* saying we must use discernment to understand ourselves, and then use denial as we reject the immoral urge and renounce any illegal actions.

The dynamics for all this is the Holy Spirit. "The fruit of the Spirit is love, joy, peace . . . and self-control" (Gal. 5: 22,23 RSV). As we write these principles of action deep upon our hearts, we will learn to live by the Spirit in the crucial area of our sexuality.

10

The Christian

and Divorce

> It hath been said, Whosoever shall put away his wife, let him give her a writing of divorcement: But I say unto you, That whosoever shall put away his wife, saving for the cause of fornication, causeth her to commit adultery: and whosoever shall marry her that is divorced committeth adultery (Matt. 5:31,32).

We cannot discuss divorce without dealing further with the whole topic of marriage, the subject of the previous chapter. It is interesting to note that Jesus refused to be trapped into talking about divorce. Rather, he felt that the important thing to talk about was marriage:

> And the Pharisees came to him, and asked him, Is it lawful for a man to put away his wife? tempting him. And he answered ... them, What did Moses command you? And they said, Moses suffered to write a bill of divorcement, and to put her away. And Jesus answered and said unto them, For the hardness of your heart he wrote you this precept. But from the beginning of the creation God made them male and female. For this cause shall a man leave his father and mother, and cleave to his wife; and they twain shall be one flesh: so then they are no more twain, but one flesh. What therefore God hath joined together, let not man put asunder.... Whosoever shall put

away his wife, and marry another, committeth adultery against her. And if a woman shall put away her husband, and be married to another, she committeth adultery (Mark 10:2–12).

I have found in my own marriage counseling experience that often people come to me to talk about divorce, only because they are so ignorant about marriage. Our need in today's world is not for a more enlightened approach to divorce, but for a stronger presentation of the biblical principles of marriage. One of modern society's greatest disaster areas is marital and family breakdown, the disintegration of the family unit. What is needed is an authoritative statement from the Scriptures regarding this all-important aspect of life. The Bible's teaching on this subject of divorce is diametrically opposed to the teachings of society. Secular philosophy and scriptural truth are incompatible, yet in the church today too many of us are secular in our attitude toward divorce.

As we look at this matter of divorce together, I have chosen to divide the discussion under three broad headings: a serious situation, a searching statement, and a spiritual solution.

A Serious Situation

Right in the middle of his discussion of behavior patterns for Christians, the Lord Jesus suddenly launches into a discourse on divorce, indicating something of the seriousness of this problem. Really, it doesn't seem to fit the context of the rest of his teachings. Obviously, his purpose in discussing divorce at this point is to impress upon his hearers the sanctity of the family relationship. They were in extreme danger of absorbing the secular philosophy so prevalent around them. First of all, this attitude toward divorce was so liberal that we might almost call it "legalized adultery." The abuse of the divorce principle enunciated in the Scriptures is out of the question for the Christian. In re-reading the scriptures concerning the original institution of marriage, I was impressed with its application, not to Adam and Eve, the first married couple, but to us, their descendants. Genesis 2:24 spells it out for us: "Therefore shall a man leave his father and his mother, and shall cleave unto his wife: and they shall be one flesh." Adam and Eve had no mother or father, so this statement was not made for their benefit. It sets up the scriptural principle of commitment to one another which a married couple is to make. Because this is a biblical principle, therefore, whom God has joined together, let no man put asunder (Matt. 19:6). These are the words of Jesus, not man's words. And because we ignore their solemnity, the institution of marriage is in serious trouble today, as it was in Jesus' day.

Compare the condition of women in Jesus' day to their condition in the Old Testament: "When a man hath taken a wife, and married her, and it come to pass that she find no favor in his eyes, because he hath found some uncleanness in her: then let him write her a bill of divorcement, and give it in her hand, and send her out of his house" (Deut. 24:1). This is the Old Testament statement of the divorce principle. The woman is chattel: she is nothing but a piece of property, with no rights at all, no better indeed than a slave. For no reason at all, a man could divorce his wife. If she displeased him in any way, this was his way of escape. The stipulation that some "uncleanness" must be found in her had gone by the board. The Old Testament required that some sexual misconduct be involved before this action could be allowed, but the Jews had conveniently overlooked that aspect and used this law as an excuse for divorce on any grounds. This was the attitude Jesus was condemning in his statement on the subject.

Is divorce a problem in the United States? You be the judge. There were 264,000 divorces in the United States in 1940. By 1950 the figure had risen to 385,000. By 1960 it was up to 393,000. The figure for 1970 was 715,000. We have now passed the 1,000,000 mark. From a quarter of a million divorces to more than a million divorces in less than forty years would indicate to me that we have an escalating divorce problem in this country of ours.

Not only do we have an escalating problem, we also have an erosion of principles. In the state where I have a pastorate (Wisconsin) the following grounds are admissible for divorce: adultery; physical or mental cruelty; incompatibility; desertion; alcoholism; impotency; non-support; insanity; pregnancy at marriage; bigamy; separation or absence; felony conviction or imprisonment; drug addiction; fraud, force, or duress; prior decree of limited divorce. This is not even an exhaustive list, but it conveys the point I'm making. Biblically, the grounds for divorce are limited; but according to secularized thinking, the grounds have been stretched so far that it is possible to get a divorce for almost any conceivable reason—and some we can't even conceive.

This is what Jesus was saying in reminding the people of God's original intent for marriage as announced in Genesis 2 and restated by Jesus in Mark 10:7: "For this cause shall a man leave his father and mother, and cleave to his wife." The first principle is this: marriage is a divine principle that is permanent in the eyes of God. If you disrupt it and interfere with it, you are guilty of going contrary to the Word of God.

Secondly, marriage is a divine principle which is pleasing to the heart of God. God's standard statement when his creation was paraded before him was this: "Good." But what did he say when he completed his creation of man and woman? "*Very* good." If there is one concept which thrills God above all others, it is his divine principle of love and marriage—the development of the family unit and all that entails. That is why he made the searching statement that marriage is a divine principle.

Because of this, divorce is a limited privilege. Our world has departed from this premise so far by this time that we feel divorce is a constitutional right. Nothing could be further from the truth. Marriage is a divine principle, and the best you can say for divorce is that it is a limited privilege. It is a concession to the hardness of heart so evident in Jesus' day and our own. Those who seek a divorce are refusing to admit their own hardness of heart and desperate need for rescue at the hand of God.

Let me spell it out as simply as I know how. There is a straightforward strictness about God's law. God will suffer divorce as a concession to men's hard hearts when there has been adultery, because the very act of adultery is in itself a denial of the bond we Christians profess to have before God. Remember our discussion in chapter 9 about the three kinds of love: *agape, philia,* and *eros?* The marriage bond implies a oneness of spiritual, social, and sexual love. If that bond is broken by illicit sexual activity, adultery, then the marriage relationship may be broken. It doesn't have to be, however. God is interested in forgiveness, in confession, and reconciliation. Adultery is not the unforgivable sin in God's sight, and I'm sure he would rather the offended party would forgive the offender if that is possible.

This isn't all. In addition to the escalation of the problem of divorce, and the erosion of the principles, there's even a worse development: the easing of the procedure for getting a divorce. I didn't mention the no-fault divorce before because I wanted to save it for now! This is an arrangement to terminate a marriage without fixing blame on either party. From the humanistic, secular point of view, this is a beautiful, painless solution to a painful process. It saves money, embarrassment, heartache, harassment. If the no-fault divorce becomes the norm, one million divorces a year will be a conservative figure. Added to this is an even more recent development: the do-it-yourself divorce kit! Have I convinced you by this time that we have a serious situation on our hands? Jesus was convinced of it in his day, and I'm sure he would be even more outspoken if he were speaking to our world today.

A Searching Statement

Not only this, but Jesus also made a searching statement about this whole matter:

> And the Pharisees came to him, and asked him, Is it lawful for a man to put away his wife? tempting him. And he answered and said unto them, What did Moses command you? And they said, Moses suffered to write a bill of divorcement, and to put her away. And Jesus answered and said unto them, For the hardness of your heart he wrote you this precept. But from the beginning of the creation God made them male and female. For this cause shall a man leave his father and mother, and cleave to his wife; And they twain shall be one flesh: so then they are no more twain, but one flesh. What therefore God hath joined together, let not man put asunder (Mark 10: 2–9).

They were testing him, for no matter what he answered, he would offend one of the parties in the crowd by going contrary to their position, liberal or conservative. Jesus reminded them of Moses' decree for "the hardness of their heart" and returned the discussion to the subject of marriage.

The cause of marital problems is not incompatibility. It is sin and disobedience. The answer to this and other problems facing the church today is not a liberalized approach. It is a return to biblical principle.

It is obvious that all kinds of things can and do go wrong in the marriage relationship. As a result, people can be hurt severely. Like any other pastor, I have been introduced to innumerable heartrending situations: men who refuse to even speak to their wives for weeks; wives who flagrantly parade their unfaithfulness before their husbands, taunting them and holding them up to ridicule. Wives ashamed to appear in public because of the shoddiness of their clothing and unable to invite people to their homes because of lack of furniture. Children tormented by the sight of parents physically beating each other . . . and on and on it goes. All these problems may be caused by alcoholism. But one thing is clear—all these abuses can be rectified and all these horrendous situations salvaged if the people concerned will begin to recognize that the root cause is sin, and sin must be confessed and forsaken. But so often the hardness of heart that leads people to such reprehensible behavior precludes them from acts of confession, restitution, forgiveness, and reconciliation. "Hardness of heart" is the problem, and any solution that does not solve this is no solution at all.

A Spiritual Solution

Is there a spiritual solution to this desperate social disaster? I believe there is—in the church of Jesus Christ among people who enunciate the biblical principles and demonstrate the power of the Spirit of God in their lives. First of all, the church of Jesus Christ must expose the disaster of secular thinking concerning this problem, the secularized approach to marriage and divorce. Divorce is not a solution. All it does is create more problems.

Incidentally, let me add at this point my conviction that we Christians have a vital opportunity to serve divorced people.

The church is supposed to minister to those in need, but in this area we have failed miserably. Instead, we have ostracized the divorced person, looked down upon him, and turned our backs upon him.

We must also expose the danger of secularized thinking as far as the family unit is concerned. By the way we live, we should be showing the joy that comes to the family which operates on biblical principles.

We also have a social responsibility to expose the fallacy of secular thinking in this area of divorce. Divorce is always the product of a marriage, and marriage is the product of a wedding. Have you ever seen a couple get married with the expressed intention of destroying each other? The ideal should be to grow from the marriage ceremony rather than disintegrate from there. That is why I feel the church which is responsible for so many weddings should be preparing people for marriage and should be speaking out against the liberalization of divorce laws.

Secondly, we should be expounding the design of scriptural marriage. By our lives and our example, we should be sharing the joy there is in marriage founded and lived upon basic biblical principles of love and unselfishness. This can only be done when our solid homes, families, and marriages are being shared with those in trouble.

The third thing we must do is explode the delusion of the selfish thrill. All around us are those who are looking to extramarital affairs to spice up their lives. We should be showing them the delights of spiritual triumph in the marriage relationship, the joys of growing together in every aspect of our lives together: spiritual, social, and sexual.

There is an alternative to the hardness of heart that ends up in the divorce court, and Ezekiel points it out for us: "A new heart also will I give you, and a new spirit will I put within you: and I will take away the stony heart out of your flesh, and I will give you a heart of flesh" (36:26). A soft heart for a hard heart, that is the exchange that will solve the divorce problem.

A young wife came to me some months ago to ask what the Bible taught about divorce. She concluded she had no alternative except to divorce her husband, but I pointed out she *did* have an alternative, the soft heart promised by God through Ezekiel's inspired pen. Divorce is the result of hardened hearts, and it can be overcome by the antidote of the softened heart. "Where do I get a soft heart?" she asked, and I had the joy of pointing her to Christ. Some months later her husband came to me and said, "I don't know what's happened to her, but I do know that whatever it is, I want it. She's told me something about a new heart. Can I have one?" I said, "Let's see if we can get you fitted." We did get him fitted for a new heart, and he became a new man. The Spirit of God brought those two back together, and theirs is a happy, productive marriage today.

There is an answer to divorce and to the disintegration of our homes and families—the gospel of Jesus Christ!

11

The Christian

and Communication

Jesus lived in a sick society, and his Sermon on the Mount dealt with some of the ills of that society. Beginning in Matthew 5:33 Jesus deals with another problem of his day:

> Again, ye have heard that it hath been said by them of old time, Thou shalt not forswear thyself, but shalt perform unto the Lord thine oaths: But I say unto you, Swear not at all; neither by heaven; for it is God's throne: Nor by the earth; for it is his footstool: neither by Jerusalem; for it is the city of the great King. Neither shalt thou swear by thy head, because thou canst not make one hair white or black. But let your communication be, Yea, yea; Nay, nay: for whatsoever is more than these cometh of evil (5:33–37).

The people of Jesus' day were great ones for taking oaths. They took very seriously the prohibition in the Ten Commandments about using the Lord's name in vain, so they went to great lengths to avoid this kind of disobedience. In fact, they were so concerned about breaking this law that they went to the other extreme of avoiding the name of Jehovah completely. Only once a year was the name mentioned by the High Priest. In their common oaths, they substituted the name of heaven—or earth—or Jerusalem. They even went so far as to say, "I swear by my head." Then, because they were not swearing by the sacred name of Jehovah, they treated their oaths as not binding upon them. The result was a nation of people whose oaths meant nothing. They had no integrity; they could not be trusted.

This is exactly the opposite of what Jesus intended the Christian life to be. You and I as Christians are to live our lives differently than do those around us. We are to handle the driving forces—anger, sex, and so on—on a totally different basis than does the society of which we are a part. Now, Jesus is saying, the same is to be true of our communication. It is not to fall into the same worldly pattern.

If communication was important in Jesus' day, think how much more vital it is in our modern world! In this chapter we are going to look at communication under three headings: the power of communication, the perversion of communication, and the purity of communication.

The Power of Communication

The word translated "communication" in verse 37 is the Greek word *logos* used in John 1:1, "In the beginning was the Word, and the Word was with God, and the Word was God." *Logos* is the Greek word for the English term, "word." The identical word is used here, but it is translated "communication." The Word is the title given the Lord Jesus in John 1:1. It simply means that he is the communication of the hidden idea of God.

In our modern day this whole area of communication is almost frightening in its power, its potential for evil as well as good. It may be used by good people for good purposes, but it may also be used by evil people for bad purposes. The truth of the message and the integrity of the messenger are the factors that determine whether communication is evil or good.

One of the great powers of communication is its ability to move and to mobilize the masses. There are two instances of this power cited in the Scriptures which I would like to call to your attention. The first is found in Nehemiah 8:1–3:

And all the people gathered themselves together as one man into

the street that was before the water gate; and they spake unto
Ezra the scribe to bring the book of the law of Moses, ... And
Ezra the priest brought the law before the congregation both of
men and women, and all that could hear with understanding,
upon the first day of the seventh month. And he read therein
before the street that was before the water gate from the morning until midday, ... and the ears of all the people were atten-
tive unto the book of the law.

Following this mass meeting of Israel to hear the Word of
God, the people rallied around to rebuild the city of Jerusalem. This is a beautiful illustration of the power of communication to cause a revival among a people who had wandered
far from the place God has planned for them. They rose up
and confessed their sin—and the nation began to move toward
God and for God once more. This is an example of the power
of communication.

Joshua offers us another illustration. The children of Israel
had been wandering for forty years in the wilderness, and now
they were on the brink of the Jordan, waiting to cross over
against the city of Jericho. "And Joshua said unto the people,
Sanctify yourselves: for to-morrow the Lord will do wonders
among you" (Josh 3:5). Joshua shared with the people what
God had told him about the taking of Jericho, and the next
day saw Israel enjoy a thrilling triumph over their enemies.

There is no question about it—communication is a tremendously powerful force. There are examples outside of the
Bible to back up this premise. Think of the powerful simplic-
ity of the Gettysburg Address, the short speech made by
President Lincoln dedicating the national cemetery at Gettysburg, Pennsylvania. It will continue to live in our memories as
long as the world continues, I'm sure.

The evil that can come out of communication is best il-
lustrated by the striking story of Adolph Hitler, the inhuman
dictator of Germany whose dark designs plunged the world
into World War II. Whatever your attitude toward the man
Hitler, you must admit his effectiveness as a communicator.
He swept an entire nation behind him by the power of his
voice. We may not agree with what he was communicating,
but we cannot argue the fact that he was an effective communicator.

I, of course, cannot help but mention another effective communicator of that same period in history: Winston Churchill. He successfully motivated a nation without sufficient weaponry to stand against the tide of Nazi aggression. I can remember Churchill's speeches and his unsurpassed ability to motivate and mobilize a tired and war-weary people. A man like Martin Luther King shames me, when I see how effectively he communicated to the masses. Whatever you may think of the man, you cannot deny his ability to motivate the masses with his terse "I have a dream."

You and I communicate just as definitely as do a Lincoln, a Hitler, a Churchill, or a King. We communicate constantly. We have the power to motivate as well. Jesus is telling us to be very careful *how* and *what* we communicate. What have we done with our power?

Communication also has the power to initiate ideologies. A classic illustration of this power is found in the story of the golden calf recounted in Exodus 32. What a shocking situation: Moses up on the mountain receiving the Ten Commandments, Aaron and the people down below indulging in an orgy of idol-worship! Moses was so angered by the audacity of the people that he actually threw the tablets of stone on which the commandments were written to the ground (the first time they were broken, but not the last!). As a result of Moses' ministry of the Word of God at that time, a mighty revival broke out among the people. This is what I mean by the power to initiate ideologies.

Jesus himself is a marvelous example of this people-moving power. He changed the course of a nation, the history of an entire people by the precepts he shared in the Sermon on the Mount. We are still being affected by them to this day.

Another less sacred example is Nikolai (or Vladimir Ilyich) Lenin, Russian revolutionary leader. Along with Karl Marx he spearheaded the godless philosophy known today as communism, a mass movement that dominates more than half the world's population. These men and their followers initiated a philosophy whose ultimate effect upon the world is yet to be realized.

What about Martin Luther and his ninety-five theses? When he hammered his statements regarding faith and justification upon the door at Wittenburg, he launched a Reformation in the church whose effects are still being felt centuries later—another classic example of the power of communication to initiate a totally new ideology.

Then communication has the power to affect attitudes. I believe that Madison Avenue is having more effect upon American society today than is the church of Jesus Christ. Advertising, whether we like to admit it or not, affects us to a frightening extent. I'm firmly convinced that our appetites and our attitudes are affected more by the advertising media than they are by anything emanating from pulpits today.

Not only are we affected by Madison Avenue, the advertising industry, but we are also moved by local, national, and global politics. We are told by the President of the United States and politicians all the way down to the local level that there is an energy crisis. Some people believe it! Even to the point of turning down their thermostats! And we all know how one or two enthusiastic cheerleaders can spark a crowd which can fire a team to win a game.

Communication also has a great power to precipitate and create crises. A certain kind of music, for example, can precipitate a certain mood, a certain attitude. Movies, too, are frighteningly powerful in their ability to transmit either evil or good communication. Some of the recent box office bonanzas (*The Exorcist*, for example) indicate how this media can influence an entire nation, even the world—for evil, in this case.

Billy Kim, the Korean evangelist, tells a story that thrills me with its implications on this matter of communication. After the war the communists swept down into South Korea from the North. One of the first things they did was to gather a group of Christians into their church building, where they demanded that the leaders deny their Lord. They backed up their demands with torture and threats to the lives of their prisoners. One by one the leaders succumbed. When their torturers handed them the Bible and told them to spit upon it, they did so. Until the communists came to one little girl.

Fearlessly she looked at her tormentors and said, "You can hammer me into a pulp. You can beat me into extinction, but I will never deny my Lord!" Then she began to sing, after turning to the leaders who had fallen to say, "May God have mercy on your souls." What was the result? The crowd with her in the church joined her in singing. She turned the tide of denial that had been begun by the leaders. What did the communists do? They executed the leaders who had denied Christ and set free the girl whose courage had been so clearly communicated.

We wonder why the church in Korea is so powerful, so effective in communicating the gospel. One great factor is that there are many believers who, like that little girl, have the power to communicate their lack of fear, their dedication, and their love for Christ. But not only must we look at the power of communication, we also want to look at

The Perversion of Communication

As never before in the history of the world, communication has become perverted in its ability to shape and mold the masses. How sophisticated the machinery has become. Man can now pervert communications through what I call "Three P's": perjury, profanity, and pretense.

What do I mean by perjury? Jesus said in Matthew 5:33 that men are not to "forswear thyself" but are to "perform unto the Lord thine oaths." To forswear meant to go against one's promise, to go against an oath. It meant to give one's word, but then to go against it. Watergate is a striking example of perjury. Brilliant men have gone into court to give the impression of total integrity, that what they are saying is total truth—when in reality they are telling a pack of lies. That is an example of "big perjury." Most of us don't play in that league. But what about our handling of such things as income tax returns, phone calls (have you ever told a caller the boss wasn't in when he sat across the desk from you?), calling in sick when you were perfectly well? That's perjury, too.

I wonder if we really listen to our conversations! How often do we stretch the truth (or just bend it a little)? Exaggeration, thy name is legion! Lying seems to be the great American pastime.

Perjury operates in the spiritual realm as well: "When thou vowest a vow unto God, defer not to pay it; for he hath no pleasure in fools: pay that which thou hast vowed. Better is it that thou shouldest not vow, than that thou shouldest vow and not pay" (Eccl. 5:4,5). What about your marriage vows? Were they taken before men—or before God? What about the promises made to God in the early heat of conversion? Were they paid? What about the perjury we commit when we sing, "O for a thousand tongues to sing my great Redeemer's praise," and then fail to use even the one tongue we have to speak up for him? One of the great problems in the church today is this whole matter of perjury—spiritual perjury. We think we can perjure ourselves with impunity, even before God. How deluded we are!

Another perversion of communication today is summed up in the word, "profanity." "Thou shalt not take the name of the Lord thy God in vain," is one of the Ten Commandments most familiar—and most often broken. To "take in vain" means to treat lightly, to use lightly. How often we hear the name of God used in this way: "For God's sake," "God almighty," and so on. Think of the rash of "minced oaths": "Jeez"; "Gosh"; "Golly." Every time we use the name of God for anything less than expressing his supremacy in our lives, we are guilty of breaking this commandment.

We also profane God's creation by the use of expressions like "Good heavens"; "Go to hell"; and so on. Jesus in the Sermon on the Mount is telling us to watch our lips, to watch our communication.

What about this matter of pretense or hypocrisy? There is no better illustration of this than Ananias and Sapphira in Acts 5. For their makebelieve, God struck them down. What was their pretense? "But Peter said, Ananias, why hath Satan filled thine heart to lie to the Holy Ghost, and to keep back part of the price of the land?" (v. 3). These two people *lied*. They *pretended* to be more than they were. Pretense is one more perversion of the precious gift of communication given to us by God.

The Purity of Communication

This is a better way to end our discussion of communication. The best way to clean up our communications system is to examine our motives. Briefly they are these: fear and love. If I fear God, if I realize that I must give an account before him for every idle word, I will watch what communication passes through my life and lips. If I love people, if I have God's love in my heart for them, I'll be careful how I communicate to them. The last thing I will want to do is give them a false impression by profanity or pretense.

Purity of motive calls for each of us to examine himself to see if there be any wicked way in him. Not only must my motive be pure, but my material as well. As a Christian, I must be transparent in my criticism of those who are guilty of profanity and pretense. Let's not call it sophisticated or simplistic. Tell it like it is by consistency of life and lip. We Christians must take our stand as did the little girl in the Korean church. Stand up and be counted! Don't deny God by quietly standing by when his name is besmirched and belittled.

Purity of method is vital if we are to clean up our communications system. We must check Psalm 51 to examine our actions and evaluate our commitment. "Create in me a clean heart, O God; and renew a right spirit within me," we must pray with David (v. 10). We must use James 3 as a thermometer to eradicate any inconsistency in our lives that will hinder God's working through us to minister to others.

Communication is the name of the game. What does my life communicate—life and love, or death and hate? May I move the masses with whom I communicate toward the Savior—not away from him!

12

The Christian
and Relationships

One of the greatest problems confronting modern society is the failure of societal members to relate to one another. Jesus had a strong statement on this matter:

> Ye have heard that it hath been said, An eye for an eye, and a tooth for a tooth: But I say unto you, That ye resist not evil: but whosoever shall smite thee on thy right cheek, turn to him the other also. And if any man will sue thee at the law, and take away thy coat, let him have thy cloak also. And whosoever shall compel thee to go a mile, go with him twain. Give to him that asketh thee, and from him that would borrow of thee turn not thou away (Matt. 5:38–42).

John Donne said, "No man is an island." Isolationism is impossible. No human being can be totally self-sufficient and thoroughly self-contained. For very obvious reasons, we are all members of society, and because we are, we're interrelated and interdependent.

Let's examine what Jesus was saying in this passage. First of all, the relationships of which he speaks operate within his kingdom. Unfortunately, we realize that the king of this world is not the Lord Jesus Christ. The Bible teaches that Satan has this old world in his grip. Many of the institutions and organizations in our world today are not the product of the kingship of Jesus Christ. He is not the author of our problems. These are the products of the kingship of Satan. This is why we sometimes encounter problems. As Christians we are members of the kingdom of God, but as human beings we must live in a world dominated by Satan. Thus we are constantly confronted with conflict. How does a person who is a member of the kingdom of God function in a society manipulated not by the God whom he worships, but by a ruler in total opposition to the One whom he supports? That is the crux of the Christian's constant conflict. It is important that we understand this because as we look at some of the issues that Jesus Christ speaks to here, we would run into some terrible problems if we tried to put them into operation in some of the secular areas in which we're required to work and live.

How should we apply the statement in verse 39, "resist not evil"? Some believers feel very strongly that this command applies to the nations of the world. A significant segment of the church feels that this principle if built into international relations would produce world peace. But to achieve that glorious end requires nothing less than the agreement of all parties—not a very promising prospect! Is it likely that Hitler would have been stopped by the turned cheeks of a million Jews?

We must be careful, however, not to go to the other extreme. Many people have chosen to ignore the principles entirely. This attitude cannot be right because Christ never taught in order that he might be ignored! I believe in this passage there are principles that we can neither ignore nor can we impose them on a godless world. Rather, we must apply them as Christians in our life style as members of the kingdom of God on earth. This will be the burden of this chapter. We will consider relationship potential, relationship pollution, and relationship principles.

Relationship Potential

As I've already pointed out, no man is an island. We're all members of society, and therefore the basis on which we operate is a relational basis. We are relational beings. The relationships we build have either tremendous potential for development, or they have terrible possibilities for destruction. The right kind of relationship can bring about great growth, a beautiful expansion of personality—and the wrong kind of relationship can create chaos, the literal destruction of personhood.

Scripture is full of illustrations of healthy, helpful relationships. Look at an unlikely pair like Saul and Barnabas. Remember how suspicious the early church people were of the newly converted Saul. Only Barnabas welcomed him with open arms, and God worked miracles through that relationship. Saul of Tarsus had been a hothead, a persecutor of the Christians. Barnabas was known as the son of consolation. What a beautiful person he must have been. As a result of these two, totally *different* people being brought together, the church gained a whole new vision of its place in God's plan and program. Barnabas was the encourager, the supporter, Paul, the initiator, the spokesman.

As Christians, every one of us needs relationships. We need people with whom we can unburden ourselves, with whom we can simply *be* ourselves. It is vitally important that you and I as Christians be involved in relationships that build up people in every dimension.

As I think back upon my own life, I remember with gratitude certain people who had a tremendous influence upon me. First of all, my parents left their mark upon me, shaping my early life. In the business world, several outstanding men had their effect upon me. I remember my immediate superior in the bank where I first worked. What a disciplinarian he was. As a young bank teller, I had great fear of that man, for he insisted that my accounts must balance every night before I could go home. But the discipline and determination in his life were growing experiences for me. Later on, there were many great men of God whose lives influenced mine in the ministry.

You and I are relational people. We are either expanded or constricted by those with whom we go through life. And of course we have similar impact on them. Are we encouragers like Barnabas and Jonathan? Or do we destroy those closest to us? Unfortunately, there are people whose aim seems to be to rip the other person apart. Sometimes even husbands and wives reach this kind of an impasse in the marriage relationship—or parents and children seem intent upon destructive rather than constructive relationships. People within the same church fellowship can get into this kind of situation as well.

These destructive relationships result in the destruction of the objectives of people with whom we should be building positive ties. They also result in the denial of opportunities for growth and development. This ultimately culminates in the complete disintegration of that other person, so far as the original relationship is concerned. If you or I have ever had such a negative or destructive relationship with another person, that breach must be healed and the rebuilding process must begin. We must first of all ask God for forgiveness, and then go to the person we have wronged and ask for his forgiveness.

Relationship Pollution

We live in a nation built on the conviction that people have certain inalienable rights. This premise in itself must lead to ultimate conflict. Somewhere along the way your inalienable rights and mine are going to come into conflict or confrontation. I realize that I may sound unpatriotic and un-American, but the fact remains that this "great American philosophy" can lead to a fragmented society.

Think of the potential problem in the marriage relationship if both partners insist upon their rights. Such a concern for human rights can lead a man into pretty direct conflict with his wife. And the same is true in any business relationships we might discuss. Have you ever worked with someone who insisted on his right to be treated with dignity? He's so prickly that only a select few can associate with him. This is the kind of man who would question Jesus' statement in verse 39: ". . . whosoever shall smite thee on thy right cheek, turn to him the other also." Such a person would, rather than turn the other cheek, retort, "After all, I have my rights," and lash back.

Beside those who say, "Don't insult my dignity," there are those who insist, "Don't interfere with my security." These are the people to whom Jesus was speaking in verse 40: "And if any man will sue thee at the law, and take away thy coat, let him have thy cloak also." What is the normal reaction when one is faced with a suit like this? Hire the best attorney you can find. But Jesus was literally suggesting that his Jewish brethren (and those of us who claim to be his spiritual brethren) give up not only our garments but even our "security blanket" (the cloak was used by the Jews as a blanket at night) rather than risk severing a relationship. That was a revolutionary idea in his day, and in our day as well. One of our inalienable rights, we feel, is the right to our own security. This lies behind our idea that we have the right to carry arms to protect our homes and loved ones, the basic idea that "I have the right to secure my situation." What carnage could result if this philosophy was allowed full sway in our society, if we were at full liberty to insist upon our own rights. I have a right to dignity and security, but if I insist too strongly on these rights, I may end up with no one with whom I have a relationship!

Jesus dealt with another of these "inalienable" rights: the right to privacy. "And whosoever shall compel thee to go a mile, go with him twain" (v. 41). You will remember Jesus was speaking to a group of people at the complete mercy of the Roman soldiery. It was quite common for these rough Roman soliders to use Jews as their beasts of burden—to compel them to carry their loads. A good example of this is Simon of Cyrene, who was compelled to carry Jesus' cross. It wasn't his idea. He was drafted. Suppose you had received complimentary tickets to a ball game to be played this evening, but your boss wanted you to work overtime. That would be an invasion of your privacy! And you'd be reluctant to let it happen. Insisting on your rights might not have the desired effect upon your relationship with your boss—but gladly surrendering your right to privacy would be a different story!

In verse 42 Jesus dealt with another right: "Give to him that asketh thee, and from him that would borrow of thee turn not away." Now he is touching on our basic right to preserve our own property. Our natural instinct is to protect our own property, but Jesus is telling us to give up that right in this remarkable command.

What was Jesus saying? In modern terminology, I believe

he said, "If you want to pollute a relationship, here's how you do it: Insist on no one insulting your dignity. Make sure no one interferes with your security. Protect your privacy at all costs. And don't let anyone infringe on your property rights." These four areas are at the root of most of our societal problems today.

Another way to pollute a relationship is the practice of reaction. In every area so far discussed, Jesus was looking at the possibility of reaction—normal reaction. What's the normal reaction when someone strikes you? To strike back, of course. That's how and why wars are fought. Reaction is automatic. But what does it do to relationships? It shatters them.

What is Jesus suggesting? The Hebrew law allowed "a tooth for a tooth, and an eye for an eye." That was a limitation the law laid down. People seem to interpret this as "getting even" whenever you are wronged. It was not so much a mandate to get his tooth if he got yours—but rather an insistence that if you must react to his action your reaction must be no greater than his action. Rather, it is a limitation. No more than one tooth for one tooth! The Israelis live by this law even today. If one of their aircraft is blown up, you can count on it: an enemy aircraft will go up in smoke within a few days somewhere in Rome or Athens, Lebanon or Egypt. But Jesus is urging something different. He says, "Don't simply work within your legal right. Don't work within the permissible limits of retaliation. Rather, go in the opposite direction. Don't resist the evil that comes to you personally." Admittedly, this is difficult. Our natural inclination as men and women is to protect ourselves, to retaliate if we are wronged.

What happens when this urge to react is running rampant within a marriage? There are two people under one roof both insisting on *their* rights. There is total opposition to one another. Can you call that marriage? In the business world if management and labor both insist on their rights, what do you have? A strike, and then you have no business. This insistence on one's rights and the accompanying lust for retaliation will break down relationships every time. To counteract this natural tendency to shatter rather than build, Jesus offers us several suggestions.

Relationship Principles

Turn the other cheek. Do we take this literally? This reminds me of the old Irish preacher who had been a boxer. He came to a certain city where he intended to hold meetings. As he was setting up his tent some local toughs came up to heckle him. They had decided to run him out of town. One of them took a swing at the preacher and hit him solidly on the right cheek, knocking him to the ground. People who knew that the preacher had been a professional boxer expected him to come up swinging, but he didn't. Instead, he got back to his feet, rubbing the right side of his jaw. To the amazement of those who knew him, he walked up to the man who had hit him. Indicating his left cheek, he invited the man to hit him again, which he did. Slowly the ex-boxer rose to his feet, carefully took off his jacket, and rolled up his sleeves. Then he clenched his fists saying, "The Lord gave me no further instructions." Smack! I think he missed the point.

If we want to know what Jesus meant when he said turn the other cheek, look at his own example. What did he do when someone struck him on the cheek at his trial? Did he say, "Here, now hit me on the other side"? No, in most instances such an action would be provocative. Or such an attitude may be little more than a display of "intestinal fortitude," showing courage in the face of pain. Instead, Jesus is saying, "If they are after your dignity, let them have it. If they want your security, give that to them as well."

Paul wasn't as good at turning the other cheek as Jesus was. Do you remember what happened when he was on trial? At Jesus' trial, "he answered them never a word" (Matt. 27:14 Modern Language Bible). How did Paul react? He called the high priest Ananias a "whited wall" (Acts 23:3). Paul had his problems with this principle of non-retaliation expressed by Jesus. Let's look again at these principles:

The principle of recognition. If someone strikes me on the cheek, my immediate reaction is to strike back, but Jesus says I am to look at this situation from the other person's point of view. What is *his* problem? Have I done something to precipitate this situation? It would be better for me to examine the whole matter keeping a cool head, hoping to build a bridge rather than tear down a relationship completely. This works in the home between wife and husband, parents and children. It works in the office between employees and employer. If we can just stand back from the situation and seek to understand it we may be in a position to repair the breach rather than widen it. We stand a chance not only of maintaining a relationship, but also of strengthening it.

The principle of responsibility. In any relationship, if I insist on my rights as a primary consideration, I immediately jeopardize my chances of maintaining that relationship or building upon it. This is true in the home between husband and wife or parents and children, in the office between employees and employer. If my first consideration is my own rights in any given situation, I will doom the relationship at the outset. If my first concern is the other person, I can then begin to build and deepen the relationship we already have. Concentrate on your "responsibilities" and the other person's "rights" will be met. This should lead him to responsibility in his treatment of you and thus your rights will be met.

The principle of response. If a man strikes me on one cheek, I am to turn to him the other. Do you know what that would demonstrate? Self-control, one of that cluster of fruit listed by Paul in Galatians 5:22 and 23. Related to that virtue is the quality of self-denial. If a man demands my coat, I will give him my blanket (cloak) also. If someone makes me go with him one mile, and I go the second mile, that's a demonstration of self-sacrifice.

All these principles sum up for us what the Christian life is all about. The normal Christian life is the rejection of accepted secular standards of behavior and the employment of that behavior which is enlivened by the Holy Spirit. If my life is lived under his control, the working of his Spirit will be evident in my life. Instead of reacting blindly to any provocation, I will *respond* lovingly. When I say no to my own rights and yes to God, I am responding as a Christian. What happens when I respond instead of react? I begin to build bridges, relationships, instead of tearing down and destroying. Remember —God has promised to enable each one of us as Christians to live this kind of life.

13

The Christian

and Love

Love is one of the most talked–about and least understood subjects in our society today. I'm convinced that the reason our world is in such difficulty can be traced to this basic misunderstanding of what love is all about. Apparently this was true in Jesus' day as well, for he devoted one whole section of his Sermon on the Mount to the subject:

> Ye have heard that it hath been said, Thou shalt love thy neighbor, and hate thine enemy. But I say unto you, Love your enemies, bless them that curse you, do good to them that hate you, and pray for them that despitefully use you, and persecute you; That ye may be the children of your Father which is in heaven: for he maketh his sun to rise on the evil and on the good, and sendeth rain on the just and on the unjust. For if ye love them which love you, what reward have ye? do not even the publicans the same? And if ye salute your brethren only, what do ye more than others? do not even the publicans so? Be ye therefore perfect, even as your Father which is in heaven is perfect (Matt. 5: 43–48).

Christian love is totally different than the world's concept of love: it is unique.

In the Sermon on the Mount, Jesus addressed himself to many of the great motivational forces at work in our society.

Since love is one of the greatest motivational forces in our world, it is not surprising that he devoted so much attention to it. Without God's kind of love, of which Jesus was the human expression, our world is headed down a path from which there is no return. Unquestionably, society's problems today can be traced to a misconception of the meaning of love. We're going to look at this vast subject under three basic headings: the magnificence of God's love, the mediocrity of man's love, and the maturity of Christian love.

The Magnificence of God's Love

The measure of God's love is impossible to gauge with human instruments. In Matthew 5:45 Jesus said, ". . . he maketh his sun to rise on the evil and on the good, and sendeth rain on the just and on the unjust." What does that have to do with love? Look at verse 48: "Be ye therefore perfect, even as your Father which is in heaven is perfect." We could substitute the word "mature" there for "perfect," which is closer to what Jesus is saying. He's not talking about sinless perfection —he's talking about love, about kindness, about a maturity in God that is broader than mere human language can convey. Unbelievable as it may seem, this magnificence of God's love is intended to be worked out in the lives of God's children.

There is such a thing as family likeness. How common it is for us to say that a son is the "image of his father" and a daughter is "as lovely as her mother." Our human minds sometimes find it difficult if not impossible to grasp the implications of human likeness, but how much more mind-boggling is this matter of divine likeness. We are to be like our heavenly Father—that's what Jesus is saying here. And one of the most striking ways we can show this likeness is through sharing the love of God.

There is an image problem here. When people think of a God of love, they often misconstrue this to mean an insipid, sickly kind of love. They think of God as someone who wants and needs man's love. This concept couldn't be farther from the truth. By his very nature, God is love. He didn't create man because he *needs* love; he created him because he *is* love.

In a sense, this truth is what Jesus was pointing out when he reminded his hearers that God made the sun and causes it to shine on all men. He made everything, but the sun is one of the most beautiful things he made, as we contemplate its meaning to our world. He not only made it, he shares it with us. If he didn't, where would this world be? Whose sun is it? *His* sun, says Jesus here. That's the essence of his love.

What does that mean for me? If I'm to represent him here, I must share that love, too. There is no such thing as selfish, me-first love. Love by its very nature must share.

Not only does he *share* his love, he also *sends* it. Notice the next phrase in the verse, " . . . and sendeth rain on the just and on the unjust." "For God so loved the world, that he gave his only . . . Son, that whosoever believeth in him should not perish, but have everlasting life" (John 3:16). No one verse better epitomizes the full-orbed meaning of God's love than this brief, beloved sentence. As he talks to his audience on the Mount, Jesus is saying in essence, "If you want to do anything in the world, if you are going to make any kind of a meaningful impact, then you must understand this: you are going to have to be children of your Father, reflecting his nature—and his nature is *giving* love."

The magnificence of God's love is not only according to God's nature which we have been tracing thus far, it is also according to man's need. God has tremendous resources—the sun and the rain are just a part of his creation. And he is ready and waiting to share those resources. Look around us today. Who is taking credit for the energy resources surrounding us? Man. Who is messing things up? Man. Who's really in control? God. "The earth is the Lord's and the fullness thereof" (Ps. 24:1). Fullness of what? Fullness of oil, coal, and all the other forms of energy we men call ours. God loves according to need, not according to character. The sun and the rain are available to the evil and the good. How thankful we should be for that fact! If our goodness determined the measure of his blessing, how impoverished we would be. If it was up to man to apportion out the rain and sun, only a select few would enjoy such benefits. But that's not the way of God's love. Human love responds to a character of which we approve. God's love comes *in spite* of character, not *because of*. This is the magnificence of God's love, but now let's look at

The Mediocrity of Man's Love

The first thing about man's love that makes it mediocre is that man reserves the right to hate. We've looked at man's rights before in this book, and you will recall that insistence upon one's rights is what breaks down relationships. As human beings, we feel we have an inalienable right to reject certain people. This is why we know so little about the love of God. The love of God doesn't hate people—it hates what they do. Still he sends his sun and rain upon all, the unjust and the just. If we were in charge of dispensing rain and sunshine, we would be tempted to share them only with those we love. That's the way we operate, and that's why our love is medio-cre.

How many of us are guilty of wishing evil upon another person? Two of us are in line for a job. The other person falls and breaks his leg, so I get the position. Do I feel sorry—or secretly glad about my good fortune and his misfortune? Or that one who seems to have everything life could offer—and then loses it. Am I genuinely sorry for him, or secretly glad that he's down where I live now? Human love reserves the right to wish evil upon another, but divine love never does.

"Bless them that curse you, do good to them that hate you, and pray for them which despitefully use you, and persecute you." How foreign such actions are to the human spirit. That's why we need an injection of the Holy Spirit! In Jesus' day as now, people insisted upon their rights to hate, to reject, to "despitefully use." But Jesus called them to melt their hard hearts, their frozen attitudes, and begin to react in love.

Peter touched on this in his first Epistle: "Having a good conscience; that, whereas they speak evil of you, as of evildoers, they may be ashamed that falsely accuse your good conversation in Christ" (3:16). This is what it means to "despitefully use" another person. If you and I want others to believe we are children of our heavenly Father, we must be above such behavior, even though the world around us indulges in it.

Jesus also spoke of those who persecute us. That means those who apply pressure, who grind others into the dirt if they get the chance. Of all people, Christians are not to be guilty of that kind of conduct. The fact that we can slip into it at a moment's notice is the reason human love is so mediocre. If you are going to be God's person, you cannot settle for mediocre love—you insist on magnificent love.

The publicans to whom Jesus referred in verse 46—"For if ye love them which love you, what reward have ye? do not even the publicans the same?"—were tax collectors. In the Roman world these men were the lowest of the low. They were traitors to their countrymen, parasites who bled their countrymen white. Tax collectors didn't have to turn over all they collected. Provided they remitted the required amount to headquarters no one asked any questions about how much more than that amount they were extorting. So they "took" their fellow Jews for all they could to feather their own nests. Jesus pointed out that even men as low on the societal scale as this could love their own kind. Evidently there was love among rogues in the same way there is honor among thieves!

This is one of the most telling criticisms of the church today —our lack of love for those unlike us. Christian love doesn't only extend to those just like me. It is supposed to extend to all men! The watching world looks at the church and sees how "we love one another"—but they fail to see much evidence of our love for those outside the church. Because we restrict our love to certain attitudes, special associations, and limited activities, we show only a mediocre human love instead of

The Maturity of Christian Love

What are the *demands* of God upon the Christian? "Thou shalt love the Lord thy God with all thy heart, and with all thy soul, and with all thy strength, and with all thy mind; and thy neighbor as thyself" (Luke 10:27). First and foremost, we are to love God—emotionally (heart and soul), intellectually (mind), and physically (strength). That pretty well touches on every area, doesn't it? The second major demand is that we love our neighbors as ourselves. Have we ever realized that God loves other people as much as he loves us? It came home to me one day that God had made a world full of unique individuals, and he loved every one of them just as much as he loved me. I am only one among millions.

What am I trying to say? It's perfectly biblical to love oneself and consider oneself unique and special. But I am not to be self–centered and selfish. I also have the responsibility to realize that other people are special, too. I am to love them as much as I love myself. God has given me a certain sphere of influence and a certain set of gifts, and I am to function in that sphere and use those gifts for others. His demands are simply this: love me and love your neighbor, in that order. Not only that—the uniqueness of the Christian position is that I'm to love my enemy too!

Do you know what is going to happen to our world? If there is not a revival of the church of Jesus Christ that begins to produce men and women who really love with this all-consuming love of God, society is going to disintegrate. Love God, yourself, and others (including your enemies). That's the divine demand.

We are also called upon to *display* our love. How do I display my love for God? By my obedience to his commands. How do I show my love to others? Read the story of the Good Samaritan. Who is my neighbor? The man in the ditch whose body has been battered, whose life has been almost snuffed out by robbers, the man who *needs* me. If I ignore him as did the Levite and the priest, in what way am I different than the rest of the world? But if I minister to his needs as I would to my own, then I am showing divine love. How do I show this love? By sacrifice. It's not an easy kind of love. How do I show love to those who hate me, who misuse me? By the way I react to them in love. That's not an easy love, either.

That leads me to the *dynamics* of Christian love.

Where does this kind of love come from? Do I whip it up in myself? Does it come from within me? The force of Christian love comes from *the dynamic of divine example.* Let me illustrate what I mean.

Years ago the four-minute mile was considered humanly impossible. Runners had been running for years, but no one had ever broken the magic marker of four minutes. Then Roger Bannister in England broke the barrier. He ran the mile in less than four minutes. Do you know what happened? Since Roger Bannister ran that mile in four minutes, many, many other men have done it. Why have so many done in recent years what no man had done in previous years? Among other reasons, men saw that it could be done because Bannister did it. The power of example.

There is also *the dynamic of divine expectation.* What does God expect of us? "And if ye salute your brethren only, what do ye more than others? do not even the publicans the same?" (v. 47). It's a great thing to suddenly discover the divine expectation. I'm a preacher today because I suddenly discovered that it was expected of me. The only reason I ever wrote a book was that I discovered it was expected of me. What tremendous power there is in the divine expectation. Every one of us is faced with this divine expectation.

There is also such a thing as *the dynamic of divine experience.* As I experience his love in my life, I am enabled and energized to do his will. As the power of the Spirit of God is operative in my life, I am able to carry out his expectations. God makes no demands upon us that he does not equip us to carry out. I am to love God, myself, others (even my enemies). And I can do it because the example is there, the expectation is there, the experience is there, and the enabling is there. If that is true, and it is, then let us get on with the business of living lovingly.

14

The Christian
and Charity

As we move into the sixth chapter of Matthew, we enter a new section of the Sermon on the Mount—the portion having to do with religious observances. Among these traditional observances in the Jewish way of life were the giving of alms (or charity), prayer, and fasting. As men are wont to do, the "religious" Jews were carrying things to an extreme, as Jesus points out:

> Take heed that ye do not your alms before men, to be seen of them: otherwise ye have no reward of your Father which is in heaven. Therefore when thou doest thine alms, do not sound a trumpet before thee, as the hypocrites do in the synagogues and in the streets, that they may have glory of men. Verily, I say unto you, They have their reward. But when thou doest alms, let not thy left hand know what thy right hand doeth: That thine alms may be in secret: and thy Father which seeth in secret himself shall reward thee openly (Matt. 6:1–4).

This hypocritical show of piety in almsgiving extended to the other areas of their religious observance as well: prayer and fasting. These people were more interested in making an external impression than they were in an internal observance.

They were ostentatious rather than worshipful in their attitudes.

Jesus has some striking and pungent things to say on this matter. Charity, prayer, and fasting are to be integral parts of the Christian life, the life of the one living in the kingdom of God. But as with other aspects of the Christian life they can be perverted. And that is what these people had done.

Unfortunately, they had so confused the issue of giving alms that they thought charity and righteousness were synonymous. In their thinking those who gave were righteous and those who were seen to give were accordingly recognized as being righteous!

Because their motives were perverted these people were more interested in ostentatious performance than they were in internalizing these religious observances: charity, prayer, and fasting. They wanted to put on a show without changing on the inside. They wanted their "righteousness" to be on display. But righteousness is something you *are* and *do*, not something you show off like a new car. The problem in Jesus' day was that the ostentatiousness had been accepted as the real thing.

In this chapter we will concentrate on the matter of charity, but our findings will apply equally well to being genuine in the areas of prayer and fasting. First of all, we will look at charity as a product of righteousness, then as a real peril in religion, and finally as a promise of reward.

The Product of Righteousness

Righteousness can be many different things in the Word of God, but to begin with, righteousness is an attribute of God. God is absolutely right. All that he says, does, and is, is absolutely right. One of the solid foundations upon which we can build our lives is this fact.

But righteousness is a requirement of God as well. He expects people to live in line with his demands set forth in the Ten Commandments. This is where man has failed him and gone far astray from his original plan and purpose for humanity. To reconcile man with himself, God sent his Son Jesus to die for man's sins, that man might be made right with God—

or declared righteous. One is not made righteous by going around doing kind things for people, giving alms, praying, and fasting. Being made righteous is the result of accepting God's action on our behalf in forgiving sin through the sacrifice of Jesus on the cross. When a person has been made righteous he seeks to act in a righteous way out of the inner resources of his relationship to Christ.

To build a straight wall, we need a plumbline. That is our standard. To be righteous, we also need a plumbline, a standard, and that standard is God himself. If I'm going to recognize his righteousness and make it applicable to my life, then I need to reject my own *self*-righteousness. What is self-righteousness? That's saying to myself, "I'm all right," when God says, "You're not all right." My wall is crooked, but I say it's straight. Does that make it straight?

Every one of us has a tendency to revel in our own self-righteousness. We are all ready to justify what we do, rather than to reject our self-righteousness and repent of it. But that is what we must do. The Bible says that even our righteousness is as filthy rags (Isa. 64:6). The very best we can come up with by comparison with what God wants and expects is filthy rags. But realize this. Once I have rejected my own self-righteousness and repented of it, God is then prepared to give me the righteousness of God in Christ. He is ready to forgive me and impart to me a new righteousness and rightness. I'm forgiven, restored, reconciled to God. And true charity is a product of that divine righteousness.

Jesus is not condemning any public act of piety. He is simply saying my motive must be right. If I do it to be seen of men, to bring glory to myself, then my motivation is wrong. But we must not let this be an excuse to sit around doing nothing, as some people do. They have decided to show their piety and their humility by doing absolutely nothing. That's not the thrust of what Jesus is calling for here. For example, conversion is a very public act. Paul exemplifies that: "But they had heard only, That he which persecuted us in times past now preacheth the faith which once he destroyed. And they glorified God in me" (Gal. 1:23,24). Paul's conversion was so public that everyone could see it. His righteousness was properly on display, for notice who received the glory—God. We are to make absolutely certain that when we have discovered right-eousness we display it to the glory of God.

We also need to make a public confession of righteousness. Notice what Jesus says in Matthew 10: "Whosoever therefore shall confess me before men, him will I confess also before my Father which is in heaven. But whosoever shall deny me before men, him will I also deny before my Father which is in heaven" (vv. 32,33). No, Jesus does not reject public piety; he is rejecting public hypocrisy, the falsely motivated act that seeks to reflect glory upon the actor rather than God. Personal, private piety is fine—but it has to be public, too, or it will not bring glory to God.

Paul dealt with this truth in Romans 10: "If thou shalt confess with thy mouth the Lord Jesus, and shalt believe in thine heart that God hath raised him from the dead, thou shalt be saved. For with the heart man believeth unto righteousness; and with the mouth confession is made unto salvation" (vv. 9,10). Later on in this same chapter, Paul points out that the spread of the gospel is a chain reaction set off by public confession of Christ: "For whosoever shall call upon the name of the Lord shall be saved. How then shall they call on him in whom they have not believed? and how shall they believe in him of whom they have not heard? and how shall they hear without a preacher?" (Rom. 10:13–14). Righteousness, when it is discovered, must be displayed.

One further area where we display our righteousness is in the sacrament of the Lord's Supper, the taking of communion. What a personal, private act of worship this is or should be—but it is to be a public act as well. Paul again points out: "For as often as ye eat this bread, and drink this cup, ye do show the Lord's death till he come" (1 Cor. 11:26). That word show is better translated "declared" or "preached." Whether we realize it or not, every one of us is a preacher when we take communion.

Charity was very necessary in Jesus' day as it is today. There were people who were destitute, completely dependent upon the charity of others. If you travel the Middle East today, you will find abject poverty, despite the oil-rich sheiks in the higher echelons of society. Beggars abound as they did in Jesus' day. Christians have a responsibility in this area of life as well. One of the areas where we show our righteousness is in this matter of concern for the impoverished and under-privileged. How many people have seen our righteousness on display in this regard? True, we are not to do our alms "to be seen of men." But Jesus doesn't follow this with an "if." In Matthew 6:2 he says, "*Therefore* when thou doest thine alms...." In verse 3 he says, "*When* thou doest alms...." Our Lord expects his followers to be charitable, giving of themselves and their means to those who are really in need.

Remember what was pointed out earlier in the chapter on "The Christian as the Light of the World"? We are to let our lights shine. Notice again the motivation spelled out in Matthew 5:16, "... that they may see your good works, and glorify your Father which is in heaven." Those who do their alms to be seen of men have their reward. The child of God operates on a different dimension. Before charity comes conversion, confession, and communion—in that order. When that happens, the Father gets the glory, not the child.

One further point on this matter of righteousness. In addition to being discovered and displayed, it should be disciplined. One obvious reason for this is that charity can be summarily abused. Charitable acts are not a means of earning salvation, they are way of evidencing salvation. One of the reasons the church is not as effective as it might be in spreading the good news of salvation is this: some Christians are more interested in building big bank accounts, driving big cars, and living in big houses than they are in obeying Christ's admonition to display their righteousness by acts of charity. Many outside the church are more charitable than those in the church. This is where discipline must come in. Charity is more than dropping a dime in someone's tin cup. It's more than a quarter in the Salvation Army basket at Christmas time. It is an awareness of the needs of others and a giving spirit that is a product of a right relationship with God. More than awareness, however, there is a discipline of being active. Too many of us are like a perfectly tuned car with its engine idling smoothly. Someone needs to climb in and put the car in gear! What does it take to get our wheels moving? All it takes is obedience, and we've already touched on that area in a previous chapter.

The priest and the Levite in the story of the Good Samaritan were certainly *aware* of the man in the ditch, but the Samaritan was the only one who put wheels on his awareness and did something about the man's need. After awareness there must come activity. But there is one more thing that I want to emphasize. After awareness and activity, there must come a willingness to be alone. In Matthew 6:3 Jesus said, "Let not thy left hand know what thy right hand doeth: that thine alms may be in secret. . . ." Jesus is using a figurative expression here to impress upon us that what we do must be done to the glory of God. This calls for the discipline of being alone before God in this matter of charity. But charity can also be

The Peril of Religion

Do you remember the introduction Jesus gave to his parable of the two men who went up to the temple to pray? "And he spake this parable unto certain which trusted in themselves that they were righteous, and despised others" (Luke 18:9). What a description this is of the self-righteous person. They not only trusted in themselves that they were righteous; these people also "despised others." When one travels on his own standards which are purely arbitrary, he is so self-centered and self-righteous that he becomes dissatisfied with everyone around him. No one comes up to his expectations or achieves his degree of excellence. Everyone who does not agree with him is wrong—and he ends up despising everyone but a chosen few in his "inner circle."

As we move along in the parable, Jesus gives us some other interesting insights into this kind of person. Let's look at a few of these idiosyncrasies: "Two men went up into the temple to pray; the one a Pharisee, the other a publican. The Pharisee stood and prayed thus with himself, God, I thank thee, that I am not as other men are, extortioners, unjust, adulterers, or even as this publican" (Luke 18:10,11). That's an interesting sidelight. "He prayed with himself." Prayer is supposed to start out with praise—praise of God. But this man was praising himself for what he himself was. Since he had done nothing wrong, he had nothing for which to repent. Instead he gloried in himself: "I fast twice in the week, I give tithes of all that I possess" (v. 12). He goes on to pat himself on the back for keeping every one of the religious observances we mentioned at the beginning of this chapter. Since he is completely self-righteous, he has no one to praise but himself. He is a classic example of what Jesus is talking about in Matthew 6. What an empty shell he is.

Now let's look at his companion, the publican. Suddenly we realize that he is everything Jesus was commending in these early verses of Matthew 6 where he calls for true piety to be reflected in quiet, unostentatious worship. In Luke 18 Jesus describes this man for us in depth: "And the publican, standing afar off, would not lift up so much as his eyes unto heaven, but smote upon his breast, saying, God, be merciful to me a sinner" (v. 13). What a contrast! The first man prayed to himself, but this penitent person addressed himself to God, without daring to lift up so much as his eyes, let alone parade his life before the Father. What was God's reaction to these two men? Jesus spelled it out in verse 14: "I tell you, this man went down to his house justified rather than the other: for everyone that exalteth himself shall be abased; and he that humbleth himself shall be exalted."

This is the peril of ostentatious "public" religion. We fall into the error of thinking that if we give to charity, the giving becomes an end in itself. We become spiritual exhibitionists; instead of giving from a humble, contrite heart, we give proudly and harshly, judgmentally perhaps. When that happens, the righteousness of God is not operative in our lives. That phrase, "to be seen of them," in Matthew 6:1 comes from an interesting word in the Greek, a word from which we get our word, "theater." Those who give out of wrong motives are like actors on a stage. They are nothing more than exhibitionists. Not only are they guilty of theatrical charity, they are also guilty of "trumpet" charity: "Therefore when thou doest thine alms, do not sound a trumpet before thee, as the hypocrites do in the synagogues and in the streets, that they may have the glory of men" (Matt. 6:2). For them there awaits also the awful peril of elimination. When they stand before the judgment seat of God, and he asks them. "What did you do?" they will answer, "I gave ten million dollars to charity." But God will ask again, "What did you do?" They will answer once again, "I gave ten million dollars. . . ." but God will interrupt, "No, you don't understand. I'm asking what you did of eternal significance. You didn't give out of a broken, contrite heart as the publican did. You didn't do it because it was a product of my righteousness in you, because Jesus was your Lord and Savior. My Spirit didn't prompt you to give. You gave it out of a self-righteous spirit. You have your reward in the plaudits of men." That's the awful peril of exhibitionism.

The Promise of Reward

Do you know what the Bible says on this score? First of all, there is an initial reward. In Acts 20:35 Paul quotes the Lord Jesus when he says, "I have showed you all things, how that so laboring ye ought to support the weak, and to remember the words of the Lord Jesus, how he said, It is more blessed to give than to receive." Do you know why many people do not have much blessing in their lives? Because the principle of blessing is giving rather than receiving. There is an initial reward for anyone who becomes involved in charity, in giving, as a product of righteousness. The blessing that comes from such an outlook on life is immeasurable.

There is also an eternal reward for a giving spirit. Paul indicates this in 1 Corinthians 3: "Every man's work shall be made manifest: for the day shall declare it, because it shall be revealed by fire; and the fire shall try every man's work of what sort it is. If any man's work abide which he hath built thereupon, he shall receive a reward" (vv. 13,14). This scene will take place at the judgment seat of Christ. As you and I stand there, God will check on what we have done individually in the body. Wood, hay, and stubble will go up in smoke. Gold, silver, and precious stones will be refined in the fire, and based on these we will receive our reward.

Each one of us must ask ourselves on what we are basing our righteousness. Is it self-righteousness? Or unrighteousness? Each one of us must repent and receive God's righteousness in Christ. Are we letting our good works "shine" and glorify our Father in heaven? Have we had a conversion experience which is on display? Is there a communion of saints which is on display? Have we confessed with our mouths that Jesus is the Christ to the glory of God? Have we shown charity to those in need around us—whether their need be physical, spiritual, or emotional?

Is my Christianity on display, and does my charity show? Am I aware and active in showing my love for others in obedience to Christ's command? Will I one day receive my Lord's "Well done, thou good and faithful servant"? If my righteousness is a product of the outworking of his Spirit in my life, if I evidence his love as the Samaritan did, I am obeying his demands upon me. If I hide my light under a bushel, then I am failing him, falling short of his plan for his children. This is a sobering thought. As I fulfill this admonition to true charity, I bring glory to him. If I fail, then my life is a reproach to the gospel. What then will be my reward?

15

The Christian

and Anxiety

We began this book with an in-depth look at the Beatitudes. You may remember that all these verses began with the word "Blessed"—which is just another word for happy or joyful. We called it *Makarios* living. In a sense, Jesus is reminding his hearers of the truths with which he began his sermon as he now moves into the subject of anxiety:

> Therefore I say unto you, Take no thought for your life, what ye shall eat, or what ye shall drink: nor yet for your body, what ye shall put on. Is not the life more than meat, and the body than raiment? Behold the fowls of the air: for they sow not neither do they reap, nor gather into barns; yet your heavenly Father feedeth them. Are not ye much better than they? Which of you by taking thought can add one cubit unto his stature? And why take ye thought for raiment? Consider the lilies of the field, how they grow; they toil not, neither do they spin: And yet I say unto you, That even Solomon in all his glory was not arrayed like one of these. Wherefore, if God so clothe the grass of the field, which to-day is, and to-morrow is cast into the oven, shall he not much more clothe you, O ye of little faith? Therefore take no thought, saying, What shall we eat? or, What shall we drink? or, Wherewithal shall we be clothed? (For after all these things do the Gentiles seek:) for your heavenly Father knoweth that ye have need of all these things. But

seek ye first the kingdom of God, and his righteousness; and all these things shall be added unto you. Take therefore no thought for the morrow: for the morrow shall take thought for the things of itself. Sufficient unto the day is the evil thereof (Matt: 6:25–34).

Let's look back for a moment. As we have been examining the Sermon on the Mount, we have been discovering how the Lord Jesus sets out for our examination all the motivational factors that are so important in our behavior patterns. Each one of us has a philosophy for life, and we all have distinctive life styles as a result of these motivations. Jesus intended that his followers should have a distinctive life style because it was based on a distinctive philosophy of life, different from that of the Gentiles, those not committed to living for the Lord.

As a result of this commitment to Christ, we would expect the Christian to live a different type of life. He should perform differently. As Jesus said it, he is to be the salt of the earth, the light of the world. He is to stand out in the world, not to be swept up by it.

What is one of the outstanding characteristics of our world today? I believe it is an overriding anxiety. That was the spirit Jesus was addressing in this passage. Notice how he repeats the idea of "taking thought" for the morrow. Literally, he was urging his hearers not to be anxious concerning material things. The Living Bible renders these verses:

> Don't worry about *things*—food, drink, money (implied), and clothes. For you already have life and a body—and they are far more important than what to eat and wear. Look at the birds! They don't worry about what to eat— they don't need to sow or reap or store up food—for your heavenly Father feeds them. And you are far more valuable to him than they are. Will all your worries add a single moment to your life? And why worry about your clothes? Look at the field lilies! They don't worry about theirs. . . . So don't worry at all about having enough food and clothing. . . . (Matt. 6:25–31).

We need a clear definition of anxiety and worry here. There is a fine line between being careless and not being careful. It seems that some people have taken Jesus' admonition here to mean that carelessness and irresponsibility are to be the hall-marks of faith. I do not believe that is what he meant when he said, "Take no thought. . . . " But he is saying that we are not to be engulfed by a foreboding sense of anxiety as we face each day. Have you ever seen an anxious person who also ex-uded a spirit of joy? Yet both Paul and Jesus admonished the early Christians to be joyful. I don't read that either teacher taught that Christians are to evidence a fearful or anxious spirit. One of the shades of meaning in the word "blessed" which prefaces each of the Beatitudes is this very concept: "Be joyful" (see the Amplified Bible).

Over and over again the New Testament tells us that the hallmark of the Christian life is to be a joyous spirit. How can we be joyful if our souls are riddled with anxiety and worry? This is the idea Jesus was seeking to convey here. Along with freeing us from the penalty of our sin at Calvary, Jesus also gave us the key to the marvelous freedom of the joyful spirit. This joy or happiness does not come to us because we make it the object of our pursuit. Rather, it is the by-product of the Christian life. As C. S. Lewis so aptly put it, we are "sur-prised by joy" when we yield control of our lives to the Mas-ter. Joy doesn't come from desperate seeking—it comes as a result of self-surrender.

As we look into this subject of anxiety we will deal first of all with

Common Areas of Anxiety

As I've already pointed out, Paul also addressed this subject:

> But I would have you without carefulness. He that is unmarried careth for the things that belong to the Lord, how he may please the Lord: But he that is married careth for the things that are of the world, how he may please his wife. There is a difference also between a wife and a virgin. The unmarried woman careth for the things of the Lord, that she may be holy both in body and in spirit: but she that is married careth for the things of the world, how she may please her husband (1 Cor. 7: 32–34).

Notice how frequently Paul used the word "care" in this passage. Notice, too, how he lauds those who are single. So often in our day, married people tend to feel sorry for those who are single—and some single people, too, feel sorry for themselves. But Paul sees this single state as a blessed condition, a special quality. Too often we neglect that concept. But that is not the main point of this passage. The essence of his thought here is this: Care in certain areas is to be commended. Jesus was not urging his followers to "take no thought for the work of the Lord." Neither does he condemn valid concern for marital responsibility. On the contrary, Paul's thought here is that if we are married, we are to accept our responsibilities and concerns. Concern in marriage is commended both by Paul and by Jesus.

Later in his First Epistle to the Corinthians Paul touches on this subject of care once again: "That there should be no schism in the body; but that the members should have the same care one for another" (12:25). Anxiety is condemned by the Lord, but real concern for others is commended by the Scriptures. This tension is necessary in the Christian pilgrimage. Too often, we Christians pride ourselves on the absence of anxiety from our lives—but we are not concerned for others either. It takes a certain degree of maturity to have the right kind of concern while struggling to overcome improper anxieties. But concern in marriage is commendable, as is concern in the body of believers. If I lack concern for the physical and spiritual welfare of my fellow believers, I am simply being irresponsible.

Paul touched on this subject again in his second letter: "Beside those things that are without, that which cometh upon me daily, the care of all the churches" (2 Cor. 11:28). The same man who wrote, "Be careful for nothing" (Phil. 4: 6), admits here that he is concerned for his churches. The Living Bible gives this thought as "I have the constant worry of how the churches are getting along." Paul condemns anxiety, as Jesus did, but he commends concern, in marriage, in membership, and in ministry. He brings it up again in Philippians 2:20: "For I have no man likeminded, who will naturally care for your state." Paul was looking for someone who cared enough, who was concerned enough, to go on a mission for him to Philippi—and he could find no one.

Apply that lesson to our situation in the church of Jesus Christ today. What has happened to our concern for others, our mission to the unreached world around us? Yes, anxiety was to be condemned (both Paul and Jesus make this truth clear), but concern for others is to be commended.

Let's look back again at the Sermon on the Mount: "Therefore I say unto you, Take no thought for your life . . . " (Matt. 6:25). Jesus has put his finger on our problem when he says, ". . . for *your* life. . . . " Self-centered, egocentric concern for self is at the heart of our problem in the world today. Concern for others is commendable, but anxiety for our own well-being is condemned. The Greek word for "life" as translated here is also an interesting word. It's the word from which we get psychic, psychology, psychiatrist. In other words, it has to do with our own personhood, our own being. Jesus is simply saying we should not be riddled by anxiety for our own well-being.

Another area of anxiety lies in the matter of family finances. Jesus touched on that just before launching into his discussion of anxiety: "Lay not up for yourselves treasures upon earth, where moth and rust doth corrupt, and where thieves break through and steal: But lay up for yourselves treasures in heaven, where neither moth nor rust doth corrupt, and where thieves do not break through nor steal: For where your treasure is, there will your heart be also" (Matt. 6:19–21). There's one simple solution to this problem of making ends meet—and that is to spend slightly less than you make. I must say to myself, "God has graciously blessed me with the ability to earn this much, so he must want me to live at this level. I will simply live within the confines of what I earn." That philosophy will solve the financial worries of some people.

Others have an opposite problem when it comes to worry about money. They have so much that they don't know what to do with it. They would say, "The Lord has given me so much that I am worried about holding on to it." For them, the love of money has become the root of all evil. The answer to this kind of problem is to realize that each one of us is merely a steward of what he possesses. We should take the attitude that none of this wealth is ours, but that it has been entrusted to us by our Father. We are merely to be conduits of his blessing to others. Our prayer should be, "Father, please give me wisdom to know how much I should keep for myself, and how to channel the rest for your glory." So we have two kinds of anxiety about money: If we have it, we worry about keeping it; and if we don't have it, we worry about getting it. Financial concerns are certainly a problem for most of us.

Another area of anxiety Jesus touched upon was this matter of food: "Take no thought for your life, what ye shall *eat*, or what ye shall *drink* . . . " (v. 25). As I look around me here in the United States, I don't see many of us worried about the amount of food we have. True, there are pockets of poverty in our country where people don't have enough food to eat, but a far more widespread problem lies in the area of *over*eating in this affluent country of ours. But as we look to other parts of the world, we see the encroachment of the Sahara Desert, we see the awful fingers of famine stretching across the African continent, and we sense the concern Jesus was voicing here. For his hearers were facing a daily struggle for sufficient food much as do the people in the third world today. Anxiety about food was a real temptation for them.

Let me touch on another area of anxiety—fashion. Jesus condemned undue concern for fashion along with undue concern for finances and food. Here is a prohibition that hits our fashion-conscious world. One of our largest industries is the clothing industry, which speaks of the concern most people have about being fashionably dressed. And this leads me to the last area of concern: fitness. All across our country health spas have sprung up almost overnight, catering to people's undue concern about physical fitness. Don't get me wrong— I'm not critical about normal care for our bodies, for they are a God-given gift. But I do think Americans have made a fad of physical fitness. Conversely, they don't seem particularly interested in using their bodies for the glory of God or in reaching out to others in need. Theirs is a self-seeking search for fitness so that they might worship at the shrine of human beauty. Their primary purpose in keeping fit is to help themselves rather than their fellow men.

The future is also a subject of undue concern for many people today. Jesus was dealing with that anxiety when he said, "Which of you by taking thought can add one cubit [about 18 inches] unto his stature [life span] ?" (Matt. 6:27). He wasn't talking about physical stature so much as length of life. This concern lies at the heart of the current and continuing popularity of shallow and sensational prophetic preaching today. Again, don't get me wrong. I'm in favor of biblical preaching, the presentation of the whole counsel of God—but I have problems with some of the practitioners of the fine art of "snowing" gullible people with speculation and date-setting. Here again, this kind of preaching panders to the self-concern of people, which Jesus is condemning in no uncertain terms.

Anxiety will kill our joy in the Lord and restrict our liberty. Valid concern for others is one thing (commended by our Lord), but selfish anxiety is soundly criticized and condemned by him. Let's look now at

Christ's Attitude toward Anxiety

Jesus had two feelings to share on this score. First of all, he made it clear that anxiety is an exercise in futility: "Which of you by taking thought can add one cubit unto his stature?" (Matt. 6:27). No matter how much one worries, no matter how concerned he is, he cannot do anything about what God has ordained. I believe that our times are in his hand—and nothing I can do will change that.

Secondly, anxiety is an evidence of faithlessness: "Wherefore if God so clothe the grass of the field, which to-day is, and to-morrow is cast into the oven, shall he not much more clothe you, O ye of little faith?" (Matt. 6:31). I would hate for Jesus to call me "little faith." But that's who I am if I doubt for one minute his ability to take care of me, if I show anxiety in my self-centered concern for number one.

"Look," Jesus is saying, "I made your body, and I made your personhood. If I'm able to make them, I'm certainly capable of keeping them going. So don't get all concerned about survival and worried about yourself. If you believe I made you, then you have no alternative but to believe that I will work out my purposes for you." If I believe that after making me and sustaining me all these years God is going to suddenly withdraw his upholding power, I have a peculiar view of God. I am showing that I believe he can be unfaithful. This concept of God is what Jesus is flatly condemning here.

He is also saying that we can be faithless, and he uses two illustrations: "Behold the fowls of the air . . . " and "Consider the lilies . . . " (Matt. 6:26,28). I have often wondered if a bird may have flown out of some cover near the crowd when Jesus spoke these words—or if there were lilies growing in the field where they were standing. Maybe that's why he used the sudden word "Behold" in referring to the restless birds, and the quiet word "Consider" in calling to their attention this beautiful expression of his creative powers. God is both startling (as is the bird who suddenly flies from cover) and steady (as is the lily quietly blooming where it is planted) in his expressions of his care. How beautifully he cares for the birds and the blossoms—and how beautiful they are in their natural state. More beautiful than Solomon in all his glory.

Yes, Jesus' attitude toward anxiety was to consider it an exercise in futility and an evidence of faithlessness. Am I motivated by self-centered anxiety? Do I show it by my irritability and edginess? I must ask myself these pointed questions as I now take a look at

The Christian Answer to Anxiety

First of all, the Christian answer to anxiety is to accept divine providence. The passage we have been considering in this chapter begins with the word "Therefore," and while it's been said so often that it is in danger of becoming a cliché, when I see that word I ask myself, "What's it there for?" Three times Jesus repeats it, in verses 25, 31, and 34. The word "therefore" is a link between what has gone by and what is coming. It's not enough simply to tell people not to be anxious. We need to look on the other side of the therefores to see what God has for us. Let's look at each instance.

In verse 25, the "therefore" refers to what was said in verse 24: "No man can serve two masters: for either he will hate the one, and love the other; or else he will hold to the one, and despise the other. Ye cannot serve God and mammon." If I've decided to serve God and not mammon, then there is no need to be anxious. God accepts full responsibility for me if I've come to the place of saying, "God, my times are in your hands. I don't know what the future holds for me, but I know who holds my future." From this perspective I can be confident that as I serve the living and true God, I know his providence in my heart.

In verse 31, the "therefore" follows the reference to the fowls of the air and the lilies of the field. If God is able to take care of small things, he can certainly handle the big matters, Jesus is saying. After all, man was God's crowning creation. He will not let him down.

In verse 34, Jesus is reflecting again upon motivation. If we put the kingdom of God first. we do not need to be overly concerned with the morrow, the future. Base your life on divine priorities, Jesus says, and you will have no cause for anxiety. Rely upon the divine providence, and you can be confident of his provision. If you live this way, you can anticipate the divine promises summed up in verse 33: "Seek ye first the kingdom of God, and his righteousness; and all these things shall be added unto you."

The fourth thing is to apply the divine principle. A paraphrase of verse 34 might be, "Live one day at a time." This philosophy applies the principle Jesus was expressing. This is the Christian answer to anxiety. Accepting divine providence, anticipating divine promises, adopting divine priorities, and applying divine principles will overcome anxiety. Succumbing to anxiety, on the other hand, will reduce the Christian to the life style of the unbeliever. Overcome by anxiety, we lose our saltiness and fail to represent our Savior as we should. This is the burden of Jesus' admonition to "Take no thought. . . . "

16

The Christian
and Priorities

Let's remember that in the Sermon on the Mount Jesus is calling for his followers to live according to a distinctive life style, guided by a distinctive philosophy rooted in the eternal Word of God. One of the tensions we encounter as Christians is the constant bombardment of conflicting philosophies in total opposition to the truth as we know it in the Bible. And one of our biggest problems in this topsy-turvy world is to

Recognize Our Priorities

We have all heard the admonition, "Put first things first." The problem is to discover what is first. The Christian lives in a world where all kinds of demands are placed upon him. Deep in his heart he knows that he must operate on the principle of first things first, but with all the voices, all the different ideas and philosophies vying for his attention, he is struggling to determine what should really be first. It's relatively easy to say, "Major on the major, and minor on the minor"—but the difficulty lies in determining what is minor. It's really a matter of constant reevaluation.

Let me get personal for a moment. I have a real problem establishing priorities. As a pastor, believe it or not, I have had people concerned for my *physical* welfare. They have encouraged me to make physical fitness a priority. Some of the people were also concerned about my prayer life. They had been reading about Martin Luther who made it a practice to spend several hours at prayer in the early hours of the day—and they wondered how I fared in that regard! Someone else in the congregation felt that I might be neglecting my own family because of my devotion to the people in the church. Another person (who was concerned that I be in touch with what is going on in the world around me) gave me a membership in a book club!

There are other pressures on me as a pastor. Some people think I am away from my pulpit too much—away from my family. On the other hand, I have a stack of mail inviting me to speak here and speak there—wonderful opportunities to minister the Word. What do I do? How do I arrive at the proper priorities? How do I keep from neglecting my work at home as I respond to these opportunities that come my way for ministering away from home? The answer is simple—but difficult to carry out. I must *recognize my priorities.*

Some people are well-organized in this regard. They make a list, one—two—three. But you may not be that kind of person. I can make a list, all right—but then I lose the list! So our answer must lie outside ourselves—in the Word of God. When Jesus talks about our priorities, he's interested in three areas of our lives: our activities, our anxieties, and our ambitions. Let's go back to the Sermon on the Mount to discover his guidelines in this area. In Matthew 6:19 Jesus said, "Lay not up for yourselves treasures upon earth. . . . " Jesus is speaking to all of us in these incisive words.

There is no better way to measure our priorities than to look at our activities. Our activities translate into priorities—and Jesus had some very pungent things to say about our activities and the way they determine our priorities. We have already dealt with some of these matters in the earlier chapters of this book.

Our anxieties are also a gauge of our priorities. In verse 25 Jesus said, "Therefore I say unto you, Take no thought for your life, what ye shall eat, or what ye shall drink; nor yet for your body, what ye shall put on. . . . " We all have anxieties, and Jesus touched on most of them here, dealing with finances, food, fashion, fitness, and the future. The things I am anxious about are the things that take priority in my life. If we are going to get our priorities right, it is very important that we begin to recognize what our existing priorities are. If we are having trouble in our spiritual lives, it's probably because we have our priorities all mixed up. By checking on our activities and our anxieties we will soon discover what these priorities are.

The word "seek" in Matthew 6 gives us a clue to our ambitions which are another indication of our priorities: "(For after all these things do the Gentiles *seek*:) for your heavenly Father knoweth that ye have need of all these things. But *seek* ye first the kingdom of God, and his righteousness; and all these things shall be added unto you" (vv. 32,33 italics mine). This word *seek* conveys the idea of desire, the concept of intense ambition and endeavor. When Jesus talks about what people are seeking for, he is basically talking about their ambitions. Ambition is a strange and fascinating attribute. Too much ambition can ruin a person—but lack of ambition can be just as disastrous. One who is devoid of ambition is less than a person.

Ambition can be very destructive if it is simply egocentric. One of the problems in the business world today lies in this very area. People who "want what they want" so intensely that they will do anything to reach their goal can ruin lives around them. Getting to the top of the pile is more important to them than the people they must step on to get there. And these same people will also destroy themselves in the process of reaching the top. They drive themselves beyond endurance in their ambition to get to the pinnacle of success.

On the opposite end of the scale is the man who makes a virtue of scorning ambition. A man without ambition of any kind is less than human. He is an insult to the God who made him because he has no intensity of desire to be what he was made to be.

It boils down to priorities again. If I am totally ambitious to the point of being self-centered, I can blow my life apart with the destructive forces at work in me. Or if I lack ambition, I can throw my life away.

Our next step is to determine our priorities.

Rate Our Priorities

Jesus was also talking about this aspect of the problem in Matthew 6:19 when he said, "Lay not up for yourselves treasures upon earth, where moth and rust doth corrupt, and where thieves break through and steal. But lay up for yourselves treasures in heaven, where neither moth nor rust doth corrupt, and where thieves do not break through and steal." What was Jesus saying? Measure your activities in the light of eternity. Use your God-given raw materials (your strength, skills, time, energy) according to priorities set forth by God himself. It is terribly easy to devote oneself to activities not remotely related to eternity. We can live our earthly lives without "laying up" any heavenly treasure. And when we leave this earthly treasure we have amassed, what happens? It remains for the moths and rust to feed upon. And when we reach our heavenly destination, we have nothing there—we are utterly and totally destitute, having swallowed the false success story syndrome and devoted ourselves to earthly pursuits.

It may sound as if I am saying that so-called secular activity, working in a bank, if you will, is wrong for a Christian. After all, I left the banking business for the ministry. No, that's not what I am saying at all. What we must do, regardless of our type of activity (bankers, students, housewives, and so on) is to perform our tasks in the light of eternity. It is possible to be deeply involved in all kinds of activities without giving a thought to God at all. If that is the case, our activities are showing that our priorities are basically mundane. We must rate our activities in the light of eternity.

Another way to rate our priorities is to check on our anxieties. In verse 32 Jesus is urging us to look at our needs from God's perspective, realizing that he can and will supply all our needs according to his riches in glory. Our life styles and our priorities are determined by our attitude toward God's ability to supply our needs. I must live my life in the light of one tremendous fact: My heavenly Father knows my needs and is abundantly able to meet them. If I am anxious about many things, as Martha was, I will miss my Father's best for me. Rating my anxieties will show me clearly whether or not I believe in the providence of God—his ability to care for me.

Then, in addition to rating our anxieties, we must also

Rate Our Ambitions

"Seek ye first the kingdom of God," Jesus tells us in verse 33. What a superb statement that is. This puts our activities and anxieties into perspective, doesn't it? Most of us would have to admit that we hardly know what the kingdom of God is, let alone knowing how to put it first!

There are two things about the kingdom of God which we should notice. First of all, it must be *experienced*. In John 3 we meet a man called Nicodemus, a ruler of the Jews, highly articulate, well educated—a leader among men, highly respected. He was at the top of the political and academic world of his day. Nicodemus had heard of this young Carpenter who came from Nazareth, and he was interested in what Jesus had to say. He even called Jesus "Rabbi" (John 3:2), a title of respect that mirrors his attitude toward this man from Nazareth.

Jesus doesn't bother with small talk as this respected leader of the Jews comes to him. He gets right to the root of the ruler's problem: "Verily, verily, I say unto thee, Except a man be born again, he cannot see the kingdom of God" (John 3:3). There's that term again—the kingdom of God. And what Jesus said here may be applied not only to Nicodemus, but to everyone. If a person is going to experience the kingdom of God, he must be born again. On the authority of the Word of God, if I have not been born again, I cannot be a member of the kingdom of God. This must be *first* if our priorities are going to be in line with God's plan.

This concept applies to our ambitions as well. If my goal in life is to be "born again," then I will not get hung up on lesser things like becoming an All-American—or a millionaire. If becoming a member of his kingdom is my first priority, then all the other aspects of my life will fall into proper perspective.

This leads to another thought. Once the kingdom of God has been *experienced,* it must also be *expressed.* This was what Paul was writing about in 1 Corinthians: "But I will come to you shortly, if the Lord will, and will know, not the speech of them which are puffed up, but the power. For the kingdom of God is not in word, but in power" (4:19,20). What was he saying? Simply this: the kingdom of God is not talk, it's dynamite! The kingdom of God is expressed in powerful living. The kingdom of God is right here and now! It's not some nebulous something out there in the future somewhere. Therefore my priority must be to demonstrate the power of God here and now. I must not be swept up in the secular thinking around me. I must not be swallowed up by the false ambitions of my contemporaries who surround me. Rather, I must be totally involved in the *kingdom.* That is the message Jesus is seeking to convey here. If my priority is to survive in the business world, or to make it socially, then I may miss the kingdom. It must first of all be experienced, then it must be expressed. "The gospel of the kingdom shall be preached in all the world for a witness unto all nations; and then shall the end come" (Matt. 24:14). Any Christian who understands the commitment of Jesus Christ to see the eternal kingdom established in the lives of people from every tribe and tongue and nation will have no difficulty recognizing that he has a part to play in this extension ministry. And it will become a priority! To carry out this mandate, we must

Relate Our Priorities

We have recognized our priorities and rated them—now we must relate them. How do we do this? First of all, by correct application, by applying the concept of the eternal to the earthly. Jesus told us that our concern should not be for earthly treasure, but for heavenly. Are my financial priorities earthly or heavenly? How do I handle my paycheck? Have I written across it, "First the kingdom"? My checks have pictures on them—perhaps yours do, too. Wouldn't it be great if our checks could have a picture of heaven on them, to remind us to put the kingdom first? Or what if they could have pictures of hungry people on them? Wouldn't that remind us of proper priorities in terms of our finances?

First the kingdom. That means I am going to apply eternal concepts to earthly affairs and activities. If I'm going to be a Christian and invest my time, strength, and energies for eter-

nity, I may have to look upon certain activities not in terms of
what is wrong with them—but in terms of what is the point? I
can't just excuse my activities by saying there is nothing
wrong with them—they are not harming anyone. Instead, I
must ask myself what good am I doing? What am I accom-
plishing? This is applying the concept of the eternal to the
earthly.

I must also apply the concept of providence to my problems.
Is my overriding concern to protect all that I have, or am I
prepared to trust God and take some steps of faith?

Then I must apply the concept of the spiritual to the secular. Even the most mundane activity must be done "as unto
the Lord." Are my priorities in line with my eternal orienta-
tion? In my activities, anxieties, and ambitions, do I have an
overriding concern that the kingdom of God be experienced
by all kinds of people? Do I desire that his kingdom be extended above all other concerns? Is that the way my priorities
are arranged? If that's the case, I will have obeyed the admonition of Jesus: "Seek ye first the kingdom of God. . . ."

17

The Christian
and Discipline

Jesus made a remarkable statement in Matthew 7:13 and 14, an utterance we are going to explore in this chapter:

> Enter ye in at the strait gate: for wide is the gate, and broad is the way, that leadeth to destruction, and many there be which go in thereat: Because strait is the gate, and narrow is the way, which leadeth unto life, and few there be that find it.

It is not uncommon for the world to accuse Christians of being narrow. This is not an accusation. In a sense, it is a compliment. If narrow means that I have a magnificent obsession, a total and inflexible commitment to a Person—Jesus Christ—then I plead guilty! I will not deviate from the way which I am walking with him, no matter how narrow that way.

Actually, narrowness can be a virtue. Take the ground lights that tell the pilot where the airfield is. They can be approached from 360° all the way around the horizon—but only one angle of approach is right. It is the pilot's business to bring his giant aircraft in on that exact angle. It reminds me of the words of the Lord: "This is the way, walk ye in it" (Isa. 30:21). It takes special discipline to produce this attention to detail, this narrowness of vision that assures us we are on the path that God would choose for us.

The Discipline of Discernment

Some people are perfectly happy to justify their life style by saying, "Everybody's doing it." Such people are guilty of lazy thinking—complete lack of the discipline of discernment. Another approach to life is to say, "If you like it, it must be right." Others blandly affirm, "We're all headed in the same direction and it really doesn't matter what we believe just as long as we are sincere." This sounds loving and beautiful— but it is a prime example of the kind of fuzzy-headed thinking permeating our world today. It is completely contrary to the life style advocated by the Lord Jesus which called for discipline.

If we live in a society producing people who never bother to think through to what they really believe and why they believe it, then we are a part of a society which is headed for oblivion. Jesus presented us with alternatives which in turn call for discernment as we make our choices in life. Look at some of these alternatives. First of all, Jesus talked about the two ends of existence: eternal life and eternal destruction. If our thinking patterns are fuzzy and indefinite, we will not be concerned about issues such as these. Such decisions take discernment— and that quality is completely lacking in the life that takes a don't-care attitude. Simply drifting with the current or blowing with the wind is easy—but it is the path that leads to destruction. If we are going to stand for the truth as it is in Jesus, we must buck the stream, we must be willing to struggle against the lethargy around us.

Jesus also talked about two ways to go: the broad and the narrow. It's easier to drift downstream with the crowd than it is to enter at the narrow gate. What did Jesus mean when he talked about the narrow gate "that leads to life"? He clarified that statement in John 10:10 when he said: "I am come that they might have life, and that they might have it more abundantly." This life he came to give was his own life— resurrection life! Paul, writing to the Romans, said, "For the wages of sin is death; but the gift of God is eternal life through Jesus

Christ our Lord" (6:23). The Bible is full of this message: it is
thrillingly possible to experience eternal life here and now.

Eternal life is not something you get when you die if you
have been good enough. Eternal life is maturity now—being
and doing what God called us to be and do *now!* Once you
have taken that step of faith, you have been invaded by the
resurrection life of Jesus himself. Jesus Christ is alive and well
in the lives of committed Christians! I am enriched by his indwelling presence *now!* Near the close of his gospel John
wrote, "But these are written, that ye might believe that Jesus
is the Christ, the Son of God; and that believing ye might
have life through his name" (20:31 italics mine). How much
clearer could it be?

What is the alternative to eternal life? The Bible has many
words for it: "foolishness" or "perishing" (1 Cor. 1:18). "For
the preaching of the cross is to them that perish, foolishness . . . "; "lost" (2 Cor. 4:3): "But if our gospel be hid, it is
hid to them that are lost"; "waste" (Matt. 26:7,8): "There
came unto him a woman having an alabaster box of very precious ointment, and poured it on his head. . . . But when his
disciples saw it, they had indignation, saying, To what purpose is this waste?" These words suggest the alternative to
eternal life. It is possible for a person to live a wasted life, to
be totally lost, to be perishing. The opposite of eternal life is a
life headed for destruction. This is the only alternative to eternal life. In 1 John 5:13 the evangelist says, "These things have
I written unto you that believe on the name of the Son of God;
that ye may know that ye have eternal life, and that ye may
believe on the name of the Son of God." "Eternal life"—eternal destruction. The opposite ends of human society. The person who will perish is already perishing. The one who will be
finally lost is already lost. The man who will one day stand before God with a wasted life is at this very moment busy wast-
ing it. Just as truly, the one who has eternal life awaiting him
is already living that life!

The key to the whole matter lies in commitment. If we commit ourselves to God's way, the "strait and narrow" path, if you
will, eternal life is already ours. If we commit ourselves to the
"broad way . . . that leadeth to destruction" (Matt. 7:13), our
destiny is determined. The choice is ours. The promise of eter-

nal life awaits those who follow Jesus' admonition to "Follow me." Where is he going? Jesus said, "I must work the works of him that sent me, while it is yet day: the night cometh, when no man can work" (John 9:4). This is the narrow way. He also said, "A little while, and ye shall not see me: and again, a little while, and ye shall see me, because I go to the Father" (John 16:16). There is no question about where he is going.

The problem in the church today is not lack of direction. The problem is that people fail to follow Jesus. People want to avoid destruction certainly—but they are not ready to commit themselves unreservedly to the Savior. That's why the church is ineffective. A Christian is to be disciplined, a disciple who follows the narrow way. Instead, the church is filled with people who want to take the "broad" way, who want to follow the philosophy expressed in Judges 21:25—"In those days there was no king in Israel: every man did that which was right in his own eyes." The Bible makes it clear that this was the stage when the nation of Israel began to come apart at the seams.

Paul describes the same scene in more recent times: "Having a form of godliness, but denying the power thereof . . . " (2 Tim. 3:5). This is what I call the "broad way" approach to life—individualism gone mad, people refusing and rejecting God's disciplined way of life, insisting on doing their own thing and going their own way.

Christians simply must be able to discriminate and discern God's way—and then have the discipline to follow it. Jesus said, "I am the way, the truth, and the life: no man cometh unto the Father, but by me" (John 14:6). This is the narrow way of discipleship. It reminds me of my experience in Bethlehem, entering the Church of the Nativity. As is often my practice, I was so busy talking I wasn't looking where I was going. As we entered the church I failed to notice the height of the entrance. It's a small gate about four feet high. I left quite an impression in that hard rock with my head! That small gate is the main entrance to that great barn of a church. What a graphic illustration of the "narrow way" Jesus was talking about here in Matthew 7! Universalism is basically the doctrine that a God of love would never allow anyone to go to destruction, and therefore everyone is ultimately going to be saved. This "wide gate" assumption has crept into the church today, crippling its effectiveness, watering down its message.

Despite the narrowness of the gate that leads to life, to heaven itself, there will be multitudes of true disciples there. It is easy to get the impression that Christians are few and far between here in this world. Ask any student or businessman about his experiences—does he stand alone? Many times it seems that he does. We are all tempted to feel that we are the only follower of Jesus Christ in our particular sphere of influence. But rather than think of ourselves as the *only* follower, we should think of ourselves as the *first* follower— in our families, in our offices, wherever we are. That leads us to

The Discipline of Decision

This discipline relates not only to the *gate* at which we enter (our initial commitment to Jesus Christ), but it also relates to the *way* which we follow, the ongoing experience of Jesus Christ. There is a difference. Think of it this way. It doesn't take long to *get married*—but it takes many years to *be married.* Another way to look at it: It doesn't take long to sign a mortgage agreement to buy a house—but it may take twenty-five years or more to pay off that mortgage. In the same way, it doesn't take long to make that initial commitment to Jesus Christ, repenting of sin, deciding to follow the Savior. But that is just the beginning. Walking the narrow way after entering in at the narrow gate is a daily saying yes to God and no to Satan.

"This is the way, walk ye in it," said Jesus. This takes the daily discipline of discipleship, daily obedience to God's commands. In Luke 13:24 Jesus gives us a slight variation on the "strait gate" admonition: "*Strive* to enter in at the strait gate: for many, I say unto you, will seek to enter in, and shall not be able" (italics mine). Have you ever seen anyone "sweat" his way into the kingdom? I have. It is somewhat perturbing to see the "easy believism" so prevalent in Christian circles today. It seems that some people simply "float" into the kingdom on notes of sweet music, easy emotionalism, and soft sentimentalism. Discipline doesn't enter into the picture at all. Many have made "valley" commitments—but have gone back to the old ways when their circumstances were altered. We used to call them "foxhole conversions."

Such commitments lack the discipline we have been suggesting in this chapter. The crucial problems arise after the initial commitment—and if that commitment has been made too lightly, too easily, then the follower begins to falter on the way, and in the daily battle he begins to lose his way. This is what Jesus was warning against when he urged his followers to "strive" to enter in. Making a valid commitment to Jesus Christ involves daily decisions that may cause "spiritual perspiration." All this is involved in the discipline of decision: quit fooling around; give the Lord top priority in your life. This leads us to

The Discipline of Discipleship

The word translated "narrow" here in Matthew 7:14 means something totally different than the word "strait": "Because strait is the gate, and narrow is the way, which leadeth unto life, and few there be that find it." "Narrow" is variously translated elsewhere in the New Testament: "For he had healed many; insomuch that they *pressed* upon him for to touch him. . . . " (Mark 3:10, italics mine); this creates a picture in my mind of reporters pressing around trying to pick up a story. Celebrities and politicians are subjected to this kind of pressure—but so are Christians, so be ready. Another word for narrow is "tribulation": "For verily, when we were with you, we told you before that we should suffer tribulation . . . " (1 Thess. 3:4). Still another word for narrow is "affliction": "For our light affliction, which is but for a moment, worketh for us a far more exceeding and eternal weight of glory" (2 Cor. 4:17).

It takes discipline to be a disciple. The way of the disciple is a pressed-in way, a way of tribulation and affliction. Jesus made that clear in Matthew 16: "If any man will come after me, let him deny himself, and take up his cross, and follow me. For whosoever will save his life shall lose it: and whosoever will lose his life for my sake shall find it" (vv. 24,25). Discipleship costs! It means the narrow way of crucifixion or commitment. The disciple must deny himself and take up the cross. But is also means continuance, for the disciple is committed to follow Jesus—and he isn't standing still!

At first glance, this matter of discipleship sounds and appears frightening in its ramifications, in the scope of its coverage. But there are promises for us pilgrims in the way. One in particular blesses my soul every time I contemplate it: "Come unto me, all ye that labor and are heavy laden, and I will give you rest. Take my yoke upon you and learn of me; for I am meek and lowly in heart: and ye shall find rest unto your souls. For my yoke is easy, and my burden is light" (Matt. 11: 28–30). Jesus does not deny that discipleship is costly. There is a yoke, and there is a burden. But the beautiful thing about it is this: the yoke is "easy," and the burden is "light," because we take it up as a "labor of love." It is amazing what we can do when we love someone. Mothers have been known to rush into burning houses to rescue their infant children— burning themselves cruelly in the process, but not even feeling the burns in the thrill of saving their loved one. The fire was no less hot, the heat no less penetrating—but love can take the heat out of heat and the pain out of burns. Loving Jesus Christ supremely because he first loved me takes the drudgery out of discipleship, the pain out of commitment, and the fear out of following. That's why discipleship, while costly, is an "easy" yoke and a "light" burden.

18

The Christian
and Vigilance

The Christian is called upon to be alert, to be aware of the enemies who lurk around him, ready to pounce upon him from his blind side. Jesus often used the word "Beware" to warn his followers of impending danger, and he does so in the section of the Sermon on the Mount which we are going to consider next:

> Beware of false prophets, which come to you in sheep's clothing, but inwardly they are ravening wolves. Ye shall know them by their fruits. Do men gather grapes of thorns, or figs of thistles? Even so every good tree bringeth forth good fruit; but a corrupt tree bringeth forth evil fruit. A good tree cannot bring forth evil fruit, neither can a corrupt tree bring forth good fruit. Every tree that bringeth not forth good fruit is hewn down, and cast into the fire. Wherefore by their fruits ye shall know them (Matt. 7:15–20).

As we look at the alert Christian, we discover three things about him. First of all, he realizes that he is *vulnerable*. Then, because he is aware of his vulnerability, he maintains *vigilance* in every area of his life. Finally, because of vulnerability and vigilance, he can be *victorious*.

Our Vulnerability

The Bible warns the believer about three main opponents: the world, the flesh, and the devil. Because these three powers come against us with such tremendous force, they represent the areas wherein we are most vulnerable. I'd like to look at them in reverse order:

First: Satan. The Bible is quite clear in presenting this being as an absolute tyrant. People are led "captive by him at his will" (2 Tim. 2:26). Paul is specific in warning Timothy (and Christians today as well) that the devil is actively engaged in wrecking human lives. There is a personality of evil —Satan—just as definitely as there is a personality of good— God. A few years ago a movie centering on this fact made box-office history, *The Exorcist.* At the time it stimulated a whole rash of sermons on the subject of exorcism, demonology, and the occult in general. The fad is now past, but the personality of Satan is still very much with us. One reason I believe this so strongly is that Satan confronted Jesus himself. This to me is the best evidence for the validity of the personhood of Satan.

Aware of Satan's activity, Paul warns us of the arch deceiver's devices: "Lest Satan should get an advantage of us: for we are not ignorant of his devices" (2 Cor. 2:11). One reason for the church's current lack of effectiveness in the world lies in this very area—ignorance of his devices. In fact, some would tell us that Satan is a medieval myth, a figment of our imaginations. So why develop a strategy for defeating him?

This reminds me of my first experience with the American game of baseball. At first I didn't really understand what was happening out there on the field, when the players shifted their position depending upon who was at bat. But then I learned that every batter has his strengths and weaknesses— and the fielders as well as the basemen and the pitcher compensated for these strengths or weaknesses by the way they played their position. This is the way to cope with Satan. Anticipate his moves before he makes them—and the battle is half won already. Be aware of his techniques. He, too, seeks to take advantage of our weaknesses—so if we are to successfully handle his attacks, we must know how he operates. How happy he is when we don't believe in his existence at all—for then he can have a field day with us!

In the light of this verse, how can we doubt his existence: "Be sober, be vigilant; because your adversary the devil, as a roaring lion, walketh about, seeking whom he may devour" (1 Pet. 5:8)? Beware, however. He doesn't always go around like a roaring lion. Sometimes he masquerades as an angel of light: ". . . for Satan himself is transformed into an angel of light" (2 Cor. 11:14). Sometimes Satan comes in the back door of subtlety rather than the front door of direct attack. If he cannot get us one way, he will try to reach us by another path.

In addition to being a lion and a light, Satan is also a liar: "When he speaketh a lie, he speaketh of his own: for he is a liar, and the father of it," Jesus warned in John 8:44. This is he with whom we have to do. Be alert and aware!

A second traditional enemy of the believer is "the world." The problem down through the centuries has been to identify what is meant by the "world" in this context. At one point many felt that the word and the concept applied to "worldly amusements," dress standards in contemporary society, attitudes toward certain foods and drinks. According to the Scriptures, however, the "world" refers to the world system, the mind set, the philosophy prevalent in contemporary society. This broadens its coverage considerably.

In Ephesians 2, Paul refers to this concept: "Wherein in time past ye walked according to the course of this world, according to the prince of the power of the air, the spirit that now worketh in the children of disobedience" (v. 2). Here Paul is referring to an attitude, an approach toward life. It is so easy to be swept up into the thinking of the society in which we live. This insidious temptation to "go along" reminds me of a dead fish floating lazily downstream. Who wants to stand against the tide? Who wants to stand out as the oddball who goes contrary to the crowd? This is the subtle temptation against which the Christian must battle in his own particular segment of the world.

There is always a danger that the Christian may assume that his national life style is "right" and he may even regard his cultural norms as more binding than biblical principle. In this way patriotism and nationalism can be quite contrary to Scripture and in actuality nothing more than worldliness. The only way to evaluate any system is to look at the system in the light of the Word of God. It is all too easy to adopt a life style that is contrary to what the Scriptures teach. Our enemies are first of all Satan—who is a tyrant—and the world system itself, which is treacherous.

The third enemy of whom we should be aware is the flesh. This is not referring to the body as a mound of flesh, but it is rather referring to the selfish attitude that resides within people, the old nature, the power of sin, that part of us antagonistic to God and his demands upon us. Satan oversees the whole attack—with the flesh our enemy from within and the world system our enemy from without. If we are not alert to the presence of this enemy inside us, we will never understand how vulnerable we are in the spiritual realm. In 1790 the Lord Mayor of Dublin said, "The condition on which God hath given liberty to man is eternal vigilance."

In Galatians 5:17 Paul tells us, "For the flesh lusteth against the Spirit, and the Spirit against the flesh: and these are contrary the one to the other. . . . " This world is a battleground—and we Christians are at the heart of that battle! Anyone who thinks the Christian life is a bed of roses hasn't looked realistically at the battle lines drawn up all around us. In addition, the Christian is a battleground—and the warring factions are the flesh, which is antagonistic to the Spirit, and the Spirit of God which is antagonistic to the flesh. Therefore, as Paul says, "the weapons of our warfare are not carnal, but mighty through God to the pulling down of strongholds . . . " (2 Cor. 10:4). On the more personal level he confessed, "For we know that the law is spiritual: but I am carnal, sold under sin. For that which I do I allow not; for what I would, that I do not; but what I hate, that do I" (Rom. 7:14,15). Within me, says Paul, there is a constant battle going on.

Every Christian struggles through this battle. Many are concerned because of an occasional lapse back into the old life —and they should be. But they should not be discouraged, because their very concern about some wrong or questionable action is an indication of a new attitude, a new concern within them to do the right. This is evidence of the new life within.

One of the best indications that you have been born again by the Spirit of God is a growing discomfort about things that did not make you uncomfortable before. So much for our vulnerability and the importance of an awareness of our weaknesses as we face the three enemies: the world, the flesh, and the devil. Now let us look at

Our Vigilance

Here in the Sermon on the Mount Jesus is not talking particularly about Satan. At the very outset he spells it out for us: "Beware of false prophets . . . " (Matt. 7:15). A prophet does two things: he foretells (predicts) and he forthtells (proclaims). Prophets are of two kinds: they represent God, or they are in total opposition to God. The Bible has much to say about these false or pseudo-prophets, and other false people (even the antichrist is a "false Christ"). We might also describe them as "counterfeit." Jesus makes it clear that false prophets are of their father, the devil. They speak by this false spirit—this spirit of the antichrist—that comes straight from Satan himself. Such a prophet may give every indication of authority, of sincerity—but he reflects the spirit of his father the devil. As Jesus describes him, he comes "in sheep's clothing, but inwardly (he is as) . . . ravening wolves."

How do we tell the false prophet from the true? Check out what he is saying—and look at the fruit of his teaching (see vv. 16–18).

First of all, Jesus tells us that false prophets are dangerous (wolves). Secondly, they are deceptive (wolves in sheep's clothing). False movements such as the Jehovah's Witnesses come to mind as examples of the wolf masquerading as the lamb. They will come as angels of light, representing themselves as true children of God—but beware of their sweetness and light! I am not calling for us Christians to hate these people for their deception. We should love them for the lost souls that they are—but we should be aware of their subtleties and false claims. We should watch out for their divisive deceptions.

Paul had an experience with "wolves in sheep's clothing" and warned the Ephesian elders: "For I know this, that after my departing shall grievous wolves enter in among you, not sparing the flock" (Acts 20:29). How right he was. Read Revelation 2:2: "Thou hast tried them which say they are apostles, and are not, and hast found them liars." After Paul had gone, that magnificent church at Ephesus was torn apart and scattered because of false prophets. John told us how to spot them: "Beloved, believe not every spirit, but try the spirits whether they are of God: because many false prophets are gone out into the world. Hereby know ye the Spirit of God: Every spirit that confesseth that Jesus Christ is come in the flesh is of God" (1 John 4:1,2).

One of the tragedies of our day is the glib acceptance of the merely supernatural as divine by many gullible people—Christians among them. Satan himself is capable of using the supernatural. Indeed, he *is himself* supernatural. We are not to believe every spirit—but we are to put them to the acid test, their attitude toward and treatment of Jesus. Belief is an evidence of spiritual maturity—but so is unbelief! If we do not fall for every "wind of doctrine" we are showing spiritual discernment, the demonstration of our spiritual maturity. The tests revolve around the deity of Christ, his incarnation, and confession of him as Lord and Savior.

One further thought: we can also check the cults by their fruit (see Matt. 7:16–20). Their life style won't give them away, for many false prophets might live a more disciplined life than the average Christian. Their zeal and enthusiasm may be greater than the average Christian's, too. We evangelicals, because we rightly believe heaven is a gift and cannot be earned, unfortunately quite often lack zeal and enthusiasm. Not so the cultist who is trying to work his way to heaven. Another indication of false fruit is the error the cultists project, the false teaching they present.

Finally, we Christians are to be concerned about

Our Victory

The path of victory lies through the Word of God. Those who are exposed to a balanced exposition of God's Word are equipped to fight the spiritual battle that is raging in our world today. A steady diet of the Word of God is the best battle ration. It provides all-round nourishment for the Christian to strengthen him for his task.

I'm not advocating simply a knowledge of the "four spiritual laws" or any other series of proof texts to back up our spiritual convictions. We Christians are called upon to have a balanced view of the Scriptures in their totality.

The people of Laish as described in Judges 18 lost their lives because of carelessness and complacency. But the church at Ephesus in the midst of their vigilance ("I know thy works, and thy labor, and thy patience, and how thou canst not bear them which are evil; and thou hast tried them which say they are apostles, and are not . . . "—Rev. 2:2) lost their love ("Nevertheless I have somewhat against thee, because thou hast left thy first love"—Rev. 2:4). They had been so careful, so negative, so against everything that they had lost their love. What a tragedy.

The secret of the victorious Christian life lies between carelessness at the one end and extreme carefulness at the other. The victorious Christian life is a balanced approach. It requires a comprehensive grasp of the dangers that abound for the Christian and the resources available in Christ. Concentration on the dangers can lead to evangelical paranoia. Indifference to them can lead to spiritual disaster. Ignorance of the resources can produce hopelessness and despair, but a healthy understanding of the opposition and a holy dependence on Christ leads to victory.

19

The Christian
and Obedience

We have reached a portion of the Sermon on the Mount which I consider to be one of the most important in this challenging section of the Scriptures:

> Not every one that saith unto me, Lord, Lord, shall enter into the kingdom of heaven; but he that doeth the will of my Father which is in heaven. Many will say to me in that day, Lord, Lord, have we not prophesied in thy name? and in thy name have cast out devils? and in thy name done many wonderful works? And then will I profess unto them, I never knew you: depart from me, ye that work iniquity (Matt. 7:21–23).

The crux of this passage is found in verse 21 where Jesus says, " . . . he that doeth the will of my Father. . . ." It is terribly possible for a man to make a great profession, "Lord, Lord . . . " and to be involved in a spiritual ministry like prophecy—without knowing the Lord. It's possible to be a phony! One can serve the Savior without having a valid, viable relationship with him. Does this statement shock you? Let me expand on what I mean.

Obedience gives validity to our profession—and service, no matter how spectacular, is no substitute for obedience. Our modern day is seeing a startling reaction against authority, an intense distaste for obedience. This movement seems to be a natural outgrowth of our democratic philosophy when it gets out of control. Government is to be of the people, for the people, and by the people, according to the democratic principle, and this can be beautiful as long as it is operating ideally. Today, however, we are beginning to see signs of a breakdown in the process. Unfortunately, as I pointed out in a previous chapter, this kind of thinking can result in what the writer of Judges described: "In those days there was no king in Israel, but every man did that which was right in his own eyes" (17:6). The democratic system, out of control, can degenerate into anarchy. The erosion of authority can accompany the democratic process when confidence in government declines, as it has in our day. It's a two-way street. People naturally rebel against authority—and if the authority figure has feet of clay, their declining confidence accelerates that rebellion and disillusionment.

Obedience is lacking on the family level, in the political realm, on the educational scene, even in the sports arena. And in the church we have a similar situation. People in our churches who profess that God is God and Jesus Christ, the risen Lord, is his Son are also reacting against his authority. The situation is so serious that we have people in our churches who do not even know what obedience is! That is the area of the Christian life we are going to examine in this chapter. Without question obedience is the evidence of faith.

The early Christian creed set out for all the world to hear the blessed message that "Jesus Christ is Lord." This was the fundamental credo of the early church—and it implies, along with other truths, the Lordship of Christ. Lordship requires the acknowledgment of Lordship—obedience. Obedience may not be the most popular of subjects, but if Jesus is to be acknowledged as Lord obedience must be crucial to our understanding of what the Christian life really means. Let us look first of all at

The Significance of Obedience

Obedience was an integral part of our Lord's life style. It is difficult for the finite mind of man to fathom why the One who was co-equal with the Father, the One who set forth the world with his hands, should have to be obedient. Jesus spelled it out for all to hear when he said, "For I came down from heaven, not to do mine own will, but the will of him that sent me" (John 6:38). Why did Jesus leave heaven's glory for the griminess of earth? Obedience. His Father's will had supremacy in his life.

The modern way of man seems to be, "If I want to, I will. And if I don't want to, I won't!" We seem to have little concept of obedience to a power greater than ours. Man is self-sufficient and self-satisfied. But a fundamental fact of spiritual experience is this: the servant is no greater than his lord. As Christians, we are servants of the Most High God— and what he tells us to do should be our command for life. Without doubt, the first significance of our Savior's obedience was this: it was his motivation for service.

Secondly, obedience was his motivation for suffering: "And he went a little farther, and fell on his face, and prayed, saying, O my Father, if it be possible, let this cup pass from me: nevertheless not as I will, but as thou wilt" (Matt. 26:39). The scene is the Garden of Gethsemane immediately before the crucifixion. Jesus knew what he was facing, and he was repelled by it—appalled at the immensity and horror of what faced him on Calvary. But the Lord Jesus learned obedience through the things that he suffered (Heb. 5:8).

Obedience was also his motivation for sacrifice: "Let this mind be in you, which was also in Christ Jesus: Who, being in the form of God, thought it not robbery to be equal with God: but made himself of no reputation, and took upon him the form of a servant, and was made in the likeness of man: And being found in fashion as a man, he humbled himself and became obedient unto death, even the death of the cross" (Phil. 2:5–8). Obedience was at the root of our Savior's earthly life style, and he is our example in obedience.

We also see the significance of obedience in our own spiritual experience. Paul mentions it in Acts 26:19, "Whereupon, O king Agrippa, I was not disobedient unto the heavenly vision." In the next verse (26:20), Paul clarifies the content of the message he presented in obedience to the heavenly vision:

"But showed first unto them of Damascus, and at Jerusalem, and throughout all . . . Judea, and then to the Gentiles, that they should repent and turn to God, and do works meet for repentance." Repentance is a command—and it is to evidence itself in practical "works." Our life style as followers of the Master today should also evidence the reality of repentance in our hearts. Have you noticed how repentance is played down in Christian circles today? It seems that all one has to do is "make a decision," join a flock of followers moving to the front—but genuine conversion demands repentance, a drastic turn-around in one's life style, a radical change of mind.

Repentance is more than a momentary emotional reaction to a powerful gospel message. It is a conscious change of direction, a totally new life style that shows repentance. This was what Jesus was referring to when he talked about those who said, "Lord, Lord . . . " but didn't mean it from their hearts. We talk about "backsliders" in the church today—but I sometimes wonder if these people ever had anything to "slide out of"—if they ever came to the Savior in true repentance.

Obedience is also an end product of regeneration: "And you hath he quickened, who were dead in trespasses and sins; wherein in time past ye walked according to the course of this world, according to the prince of the power of the air, the spirit that now worketh in the children of disobedience" (Eph. 2:1,2). Paul puts his finger on the source of disobedience—Satan. Peter also dealt with this issue: "Wherefore gird up the loins of your mind, be sober, . . . As *obedient* children, not fashioning yourselves according to the former lusts in your ignorance: But as he which hath called you is holy, so be ye holy in all manner of conversation" (1 Pet. 1:13–15 italics mine). These two passages dovetail beautifully and call for a radically new life style no longer following the "prince of the power of the air" but instead following the "holy one." I am convinced that we cannot follow both routes. If we try to have "the form of godliness," but deny the power thereof (the Savior), we are of our father the devil—not our Savior the Lord. My life style must indelibly show whether I have truly repented and been regenerated by the power of God. If I find obedience to God onerous, and the demands of Jesus burden-some—I had better make sure that I am really in the family of God by repentance and regeneration.

Obedience is also an expression of relationship. When a person becomes a Christian he enters into a relationship with Jesus Christ as both Lord and Savior. Notice the interesting phrase in Matthew 7:23, "... I never knew you. ..." What is Jesus saying? That he had never heard of me? No. He is talk-ing about an intimacy of relationship with the living God—a "knowledge" that will leave an indelible imprint upon my life, a *personal* relationship. How do we know we have that rela-tionship? By the fruit of obedience operating in our lives. How can we talk about Lordship if our lives fly in the face of what our Lord demands? "Why call ye me, Lord, Lord, and do not the things which I say?" Jesus asks in Luke 6:46. What Jesus is saying is this: Don't confess me as Lord unless you are will-ing to do what I say. The inescapable evidence of relationship is obedience.

What is obedience? It's an expression of a relationship to the Lord, a relationship of love. If I really love the Lord, it is bound to show itself in my actions. If I am not obedient, then I have a right to really question whether I have a relationship to the Lord at all. Paul said this: "For by grace are ye saved through faith; and that not of yourselves; it is the gift of God: Not of works, lest any man should boast. For we are his work-manship, created in Christ Jesus unto good works ... " (Eph. 2:8–10). We are saved by grace, but the evidence of our salva-tion, our faith, is found in works—obedience to the Lord's demands and commands. James put it another way: the evi-dence of faith is works. This is the significance of obedience. We cannot escape it.

Some Substitutes for Obedience

One of the first substitutes that comes to mind is this: superficial worship. The word "Lord" is a simple, one-syllable word. It is so easy to say that even a child can mouth it. The problem is this: we can use the word in such a way as to make it devoid of content. Even though we say "Lord, Lord ... " we can be on the verge of spiritual bankruptcy. A superficial use of the word in a meaningless ritual is just that—meaningless. It is an empty form without power or content.

Another substitute is spurious witness. As we pointed out in the last chapter, it is possible for false prophets to arise in the church, and these are also the ones he does not know. Such people may claim the authority of Jesus and call themselves Christians, but he will have to say, "I never knew you" (Matt. 7:23), because they do not have a personal relationship with him. The world around us is full of those who purport to be followers of the Christ—but he does not know them. They are spurious witnesses.

Then there is the substitute of spectacular works. Without for one moment denying the possibility of God doing spectacular things, always remember that a craving for spectacular events is not necessarily evidence of a life of discipleship.

Some Steps to Obedience

The first step to obedience is a desire to do God's will. Where does that come from? It comes from the new nature, the new spirit implanted in us when we turn to the Savior. The old nature pulls us toward disobedience—but the new nature gives us the desire to do the will of our new Father in heaven. This doesn't mean I never disobey, or that I am always triumphant, never defeated by the old nature that still indwells me. It merely means that my *desire* is to please him, to obey him. If my basic desire is to obey God and desire his will, then I am no longer constantly demanding my own way. That is the first step to obedience.

The second step is to discover God's will. His will does not come in the guise of writing in the sky or necessarily in remarkable experiences. No, the usual way we discover his will is by letting the Word of God permeate us with his message and his promises. The Holy Spirit will inspire us and interpret his will to our own hearts. There is no substitute for the Word of God in this process. This is another important and indispensable step toward obedience and the discovery of the Christ-filled life.

The third step is a deep and ongoing filling or empowering of the Holy Spirit to *do* that will of God. Jesus said, "If ye know these things, happy are ye if ye do them" (John 13:17). Our text says in part, "Not every one that saith unto me, Lord, Lord, shall enter into the kingdom of heaven; but he that *doeth* the will of my Father which is in heaven" (Matt. 7: 21, italics mine). It is relatively easy to be caught up in the spectacular, or simply to become involved in hypocritical action, or to adopt superficial standards. But all these things do not impress our Lord. The true disciple must demonstrate his love by obedience, by truly acknowledging the Lordship of Christ in every area of his life. This is the key area, the pivotal point that reveals our true relationship to Jesus Christ. Anything else is sham and superficiality—empty form devoid of reality.

20

The Christian
and Wisdom

Jesus knew that only two possible reactions could come from
those who heard him—and from us who have been exploring
the Sermon on the Mount today. Possibility number one is
that those who have heard him will do what they have heard.
Possibility number two is that those who have heard will *not*
do what they have heard. As we look into the Word for ourselves, there are only two possible reactions. We can either do
what we have heard—or we can fail to do what we have
heard. These are the possibilities he suggests in Matthew 7:
24–29:

> Therefore whosoever heareth these sayings of mine, and doeth
> them, I will liken him unto a wise man, which built his house
> upon a rock: And the rain descended, and the floods came, and
> the winds blew, and beat upon that house; and it fell not: for it
> was founded upon a rock. And every one that heareth these say-
> ings of mine, and doeth them not, shall be likened unto a foolish
> man, which built his house upon the sand; and the rain descend-
> ed, and the floods came, and the winds blew, and beat upon
> that house; and it fell: and great was the fall of it. And it came
> to pass, when Jesus had ended these sayings, the people were
> astonished at his doctrine: For he taught them as one having
> authority, and not as the scribes (Matt. 7: 24–29).

Thus Jesus concludes the Sermon on the Mount. Now we must examine our own lives in the light of what he has told us. Will we find ourselves listed among the wise persons who do what Jesus says—or will we be one of the foolish ones who builds his house of life upon the sand? What difference has it made—this exposure to the Sermon on the Mount? Are we going to react like the foolish man—or are we going to show wisdom? That is the subject of this chapter.

Two kinds of people must react to what Jesus has been saying: those who have heard and have done what he urged; those who have heard and have not done it. We will be looking at three aspects of wisdom: it makes people sensible; it makes people secure; and it makes people stable.

Wisdom Makes People Sensible

The sensible ones are those who pay attention to the teachings of Jesus Christ. Many profess to believe the Bible from cover to cover—but they never spend time in it. They lack an appetite for it; they have no concern for its precepts. Many make great claims for the infallibility, the inerrancy of the Bible—but they don't seem to follow through with the logical conclusion of such an assertion. They fail to study the Word.

Why should the sensible man pay attention to the teachings of Jesus? Because his teachings, his pronouncements always project authority. This authority was what aroused his enemies to oppose his teachings. And this same authority should encourage us to follow him faithfully. The wise man knows that Jesus is the only One who can teach with authority (Matt. 7:29). The problem with many Christians is that they do not know what Jesus said because they have not spent time in diligent, purposeful study of his Word. If the church is to produce wise men, they must be men of the Book. This is the only authoritative source of true wisdom.

Christ's teaching also produces astonishment: "the people were astonished at his doctrine" (Matt. 7:28). Why isn't there more "astonishment" in Christian circles today? I believe it is because people do not really listen, they do not really *hear* what is being said. A wise man is one who is constantly astonished as he pays attention to the teaching of Jesus because he knows it is authoritative.

Christ's teachings should also produce action: "Whosoever heareth these sayings of mine, and *doeth* them . . ." (Matt. 7: 24, italics mine). This points up the second ingredient of the sensible man—he mixes action with Jesus' teaching. The Bible talks about two kinds of wisdom. One is theoretical insight into various areas of knowledge. But Jesus is not calling for that kind of wisdom here in the Sermon on the Mount. The wisdom he is emphasizing is prudence, a practical rather than a theoretical insight. A prudent man can translate theory into practice. The truly wise man can put Jesus' principles into operation.

There are three instances of this kind of wisdom which I would like to point out from the Scriptures. "Behold, I send you forth as sheep in the midst of wolves: be ye therefore *wise* as serpents, and harmless as doves," Jesus said in Matthew 10:16 (italics mine). Jesus is not telling his disciples here to go out with all the knowledge of the ages in their heads. He is telling them to go out and put into practice what he has taught them, using common sense in the midst of difficult situations. They were to be faithful to the Word of God, presenting it in such a way that people could understand and apply it to life's real problems, wisely handling the Word of truth—presenting a *balanced* view of the Scriptures, not a *biased* view.

"Who then is a faithful and *wise* servant, whom his lord hath made ruler over his household . . . ?" Jesus asks in Matthew 24:45 (italics mine). Here we see sensible action mixed with truth, not only in terms of preserving our position, but also in terms of proclaiming our position. Jesus said a wise man is like a servant whose master has gone away, leaving his servant with the responsibility of feeding the people (see v. 46), giving them the truth, making absolutely certain they are discovering what they need to know. Let's apply that to our lives today. Are many learning the truths of the Scriptures through us? Are we feeding anyone, motivating them by sharing the Word with them? If the answer is yes, we are wise servants, faithful and sensible in our fulfillment of his will.

One further thought on wisdom: "And five of them (the virgins) were *wise,* and five were foolish" said Jesus in Matthew 25:2 (italics mine). The truly wise person is prepared for the Lord's return. He will not be caught with his lamp empty, as were the five foolish girls. Nothing meaningful is going on in their lives. They are not mixing action with knowledge.

The wise person also resists antagonism to Christ's teachings: ". . . whosoever heareth these sayings of mine, and doeth them . . . (is) a wise man. . . . And every one that heareth . . . and doeth them not, shall be likened unto a foolish man . . ." said Jesus in Matthew 7:24 and 26. Notice the antagonism between the two reactions. The person who hears the Word of God and is antagonistic (does not do it) is simply demonstrating his estrangement from God. The wise man, on the other hand, is demonstrating his close relationship to the Savior.

We occasionally hear of Christians who have seemingly lost their interest in serving the Savior. They give the impression that they have done their bit, and that they no longer have anything to offer the church or the world around them. This is an example of the kind of antagonism I am talking about here. Maybe it is not *disinterest* they are showing. *Perhaps it is disbelief.* Nothing will kill a church more effectively than to be full of unbelieving believers. Disobedience, disinterest, and disbelief are symptomatic of hard-hearted antagonism under a cloak of evangelicalism. Such lives are built on sand, not the rock of our salvation. But let us look further.

Wisdom Makes People Secure

The apostle talks about people who are driven about by every wind of doctrine. He tells us there will be some who are led astray by cunning fables. There will also be those who start the race, but never complete it. The story of Ananias and Sapphira (Acts 5) illustrates that kind of person. But the wise man will not only be sensible, he will be secure—founded upon the rock.

First of all, note that the wise man who built his house on a rock had a secure base. "Blessed art thou, Simon Bar-jona: for flesh and blood hath not revealed it unto thee, but my Father which is in heaven. . . . Thou art Peter, and upon this *rock* I will build my church; and the gates of hell will not prevail against it" (Matt. 16:17,18, italics mine). The rock referred to here was not Peter. It was his classic statement of faith in Matthew 16:16, "Thou art the Christ. . . . " This is the rock of our faith—the blessed person of the Lord Jesus Christ, the truth of his coming.

There is a movement afoot in the church today which troubles me. It is the emphasis that we should come to Christ for what we can get from him. We are told that he rescues failures, that he makes champions, that he assures business success. This is not Christianity. This is not the rock on which we rest our faith. Jesus is the truth, and I become a secure person when I rest my faith on him. I'm not talking about an emotional high—I'm referring to an objective faith, a secure resting on the foundation of Jesus Christ.

What does it mean to build the house of faith upon the rock? It means that circumstances cannot shake it; the winds of persecution cannot sway it. The emphasis here is not on the house, but upon the foundation. The word "build" is the same word as used for "edify." Edification is mentioned by Paul: "All things are lawful for me, but all things are not expedient: all things are lawful for me, but all things edify not" (1 Cor. 10:23). The wise man is also interested in building up the Christian community. This is a dimension often overlooked in the church today. We emphasize the vertical relationship (getting right with God) but we miss the horizontal—man living in community. We are in relationship to other Christians —and we have responsibilities to them. Am I building anything? Am I teaching anyone? Is anyone being built up in their most holy faith by me? Am I identifying with other believers? The wise man is edifying people in terms of Christian character, Christian community, and Christian concern. Paul tells us, "Wherefore comfort yourselves together, and *edify* one another, even as also ye do" (1 Thess. 5:11 italics mine). The wise man, the secure person, is an edifier, a helper.

Wisdom Makes People Stable

The Lord Jesus makes it quite clear that winds are going to come, and rains are going to descend. They will beat upon the house of our lives. When the testing comes, will we be stable enough to survive? What are some of the areas in which we will be tested? What about doctrine? False prophets dressed as sheep who are really wolves can advance upon us. Do we understand the difference between truth and error?

Jesus touched upon another testing when he said, "Whosoever looketh on a woman to lust after her hath committed adultery with her already in his heart" (Matt. 5:28). Is this the area where the tempter can attack me? Am I crumbling before his attacks, or do I stand firm? Am I stable in this area of my life?

What about my relational life? Jesus also said, "Leave there thy gift before the altar, and go thy way; first be reconciled to thy brother, and then come and offer thy gift" (Matt. 5:24). Have I done any reconciling lately? How are my relationships with those in my own immediate family, those in my extended family, those in the family of God? Have I been making progress in this area?

Jesus also talked about some practical areas of life: "Lay not up for yourselves treasures upon earth, where moth and rust doth corrupt, and where thieves break through and steal" (Matt. 6:19). Am I living a disciplined life so far as my finances are concerned? Have I undergone testing and temptation in this area of my life? Am I being sane and sensible in my financial life?

Paul left us a word of warning for living our lives: "Wherefore let him that thinketh he standeth take heed lest he fall" (1 Cor. 10:12). The most sensible, the most secure, the most stable saint can fall flat on his face—but read on: "There hath no temptation taken you but such as is common to man: but God is faithful, who will not suffer you to be tempted above that ye are able; but will also with the temptation also make a way to escape, that ye may be able to bear it" (1 Cor. 10:13). Notice that the way of escape is not avoidance—but that ye may be able to *bear* it. God does not allow the testing to come into your life that you might be able to *avoid* it, but that you might discover how secure, how stable you are in the midst of the testing. He will only allow things to come into your life that you can cope with in the strength that he gives. Have we heard him speak with authority—and does he have full authority over our lives? This is the key to blessed living.

The life of sensibility, security, and stability is built on the rock. How thankful we should be for the firm foundation in the midst of a world that is floundering and foundering all around us. This is what gives the Christian that extra spark, that added impetus, to face his world with strength and stability when all around him is weak and unstable.

Christians are men "under authority" and their disciplined lives are to show it. Let's allow the Sermon on the Mount to be lived out in our lives! Where do we get the power and authority, the strength and ability to live up to the standards presented in this Sermon? From the One who preached it himself!

Study Guide

1. The Christian and Conduct
1. What is the reason we as Christians are ineffective in representing Christ to the world?
2. What are the three factors involved in the dynamics of human behavior?
3. Why does the term "self" produce bad "vibrations" for most Christians?
4. Why is it important for our motivations to be controlled by moral factors?
5. What part does our "mechanism of choice" play in the tension between motives and moral factors?
6. Of what are Christians to warn the world?

2. The Christian and Happiness
1. How does the author describe what it means to be a Christian in the world today?
2. What hinders the "blessedness" of God from breaking through to his children?
3. Where is true happiness to be found?
4. What does it mean to be "poor in spirit," according to the author?
5. Do you agree with this assessment?
6. What is one of the most difficult admissions for a man to make? Do you agree with the author's statement?

7. What three Bible characters does the author name as examples of "spiritual inadequacy"? Can you think of others?
8. What attribute does Job display?

3. The Christian and More Happiness
1. What is another word for "hungering and thirsting"?
2. What are some examples of perverted ambition?
3. What is the author's formula for "righteousness (that) exalteth a nation"? Do you agree with him?
4. What kind of people are Christians to be?
5. What is the author's definition of "purity"? Who does he suggest as people with impure motives? Can you think of others?
6. What kind of a life style does Jesus demand?

4. The Christian and Peacemaking
1. How do we normally describe "peace"? How does the author's description of biblical peace differ?
2. What areas of peace does the author discuss?
3. Are we to seek "peace at any price"?
4. What hinders peace in our world?
5. How does the author couple peace and persecution? Do you agree with his arrangement?
6. Why are so many Christians "unpeaceful" and "unblessed"?

5. The Christian As the Salt of the Earth
1. What did Jesus mean when he told his disciples (and us their descendants) that they were "the salt of the earth"?
2. What are some of the attributes of "being salt"?
3. How does the author use the story of Laish to illustrate his point?
4. Discuss some of the uses for salt and their bearing upon the Christian life. For example, how can Christians function as a "preservative"?
5. How can we as Christians "purify" and "add flavor"?
6. What does it mean when we say the salt "has lost its savor"?

6. The Christian As the Light of the World
1. What does it mean to be "the light of the world"?
2. What do you think of the author's idea of a "*continuation* ministry"?
3. What do you think of the "*clarification* ministry" he points out?
4. Do you agree with the author's statement, ". . . the darker the

place the brighter the light that's needed"? Can you think of any dark places where you are shining?

5. How do you react to the author's equating indifference and "hiding your light under a bushel"?

6. Do you agree with his emphasis on "works" for the Christian?

7. The Christian and the Moral Law

1. Our society today denies the existence of moral absolutes. The Bible provides a set of moral absolutes in the Ten Commandments. In light of this, what is the importance of the moral law?

2. What are the three aspects of the importance of the moral law which the author suggests? Can you think of others?

3. What can the individual Christian do to exemplify the relevance of God's moral law to life today?

4. What prophets does the author quote in this chapter? Can you think of others? What about New Testament writers?

5. What do you think of the author's definition of the "Spirit-filled life"?

6. What part does the moral law play in conversion?

8. The Christian and Anger

1. What do you think of the author's statement: "God's blueprint for the home is a program of teaching by the parents, particularly the fathers, which is to be reinforced by the church, the school, and other areas of influence"? Are any of these areas functioning properly?

2. What do you think of the "deterrent" approach?

3. Do you agree that "anger" and "murder" are the same?

4. Do you think they merit the same punishment?

5. Do you agree that anger and killing can sometimes be proper?

6. How does the author differentiate between the two kinds of anger?

7. How do you react to his last illustration of the angry husband? Can you identify with this problem?

9. The Christian and Sex

1. Do you agree that the power of anger and sex are two of the most dynamic forces operative in human experience?

2. Do you feel that sex is as important a force as the author implies?

3. Is the author correct in suggesting that marriage involves spiritual, social, and sexual unity? Do you agree that the three kinds of love intertwine in the marriage relationship?